Teaching International Foundation Year

This practical guide is designed to support international foundation year (IFY) teachers, leaders, and managers through all of the key academic aspects of IFY provision from an English for Academic Purposes (EAP) perspective.

This book balances recent pedagogy with practical advice on areas such as academic culture, personal tutoring, managing IFY, assessment, syllabus design, materials development, and student autonomy. Designed for busy teachers, this book provides examples of teaching materials and syllabus design that can be used as templates and chapters can be read in isolation or consulted by section as needed. Each chapter identifies the relevant British Association of Lecturers in English for Academic Purposes (BALEAP) competencies addressed within it, allowing readers to consult according to need or interest, and are designed to be revisited. There are questions for discussion at the end of each chapter, which provide reflection for a team or an individual working alone.

Focusing on the practical aspects of delivering an IFY, *Teaching International Foundation Year* is a must-read for anyone involved in IFY language and study skills provision.

Anne Stazicker is Assessment, Academic Integrity, Admissions, and Progression Lead in the Language Centre at the University of Leeds, UK.

Nancy Woods leads the Academic Study Skills for Dentistry, Medicine, and Healthcare Professions module at the University of Leeds, UK.

Teaching International Foundation Year

A Practical Guide for EAP Practitioners in Higher and Further Education

Anne Stazicker and Nancy Woods

LONDON AND NEW YORK

Cover image: © Getty Images

First published 2022
by Routledge
4 Park Square, Milton Park, Abingdon, Oxon OX14 4RN

and by Routledge
605 Third Avenue, New York, NY 10158

Routledge is an imprint of the Taylor & Francis Group, an informa business

© 2022 Anne Stazicker and Nancy Woods

The right of Anne Stazicker and Nancy Woods to be identified as authors of this work has been asserted in accordance with sections 77 and 78 of the Copyright, Designs and Patents Act 1988.

All rights reserved. No part of this book may be reprinted or reproduced or utilised in any form or by any electronic, mechanical, or other means, now known or hereafter invented, including photocopying and recording, or in any information storage or retrieval system, without permission in writing from the publishers.

Trademark notice: Product or corporate names may be trademarks or registered trademarks, and are used only for identification and explanation without intent to infringe.

British Library Cataloguing-in-Publication Data
A catalogue record for this book is available from the British Library

Library of Congress Cataloging-in-Publication Data
A catalog record has been requested for this book

ISBN: 978-1-032-15479-4 (hbk)
ISBN: 978-1-032-18258-2 (pbk)
ISBN: 978-1-003-25362-4 (ebk)

DOI: 10.4324/9781003253624

Typeset in Times New Roman
by Newgen Publishing UK

Contents

Preface vii
Acknowledgements ix
Glossary of key terms and acronyms used x
An introduction to this guide xiii

1 The challenges of academic culture 1

2 Syllabus design 20

3 Materials development 41

4 Assessment unpacked 66

5 Managing IFY 91

6 Personal tutoring 124

7 Student autonomy and its place on IFY 137

Index 152

Preface

We have been teaching EAP for more than a decade now and, in that time, we have both co-led and taught on what was a single IFY module here at Leeds, and one of the oldest in the country. At the time, it single-handedly catered for up to 130 different degree destinations and over 80 different nationality groups. Since then, the module has been split into four separate content-based modules (Arts and Humanities, Science and Engineering, Business and Dentistry, Medicine and Healthcare Professions). Nancy has gone on to lead the medics and dentists' module since this split occurred and Anne has taught alongside Nancy on the same module. Prior to teaching EAP, we both taught English as a foreign language (EFL) in various contexts in the UK and abroad and have been involved in assessment in different capacities.

When we refer to EAP, we are talking about what it means to us in our specific context, which, we appreciate, might be different from your own, but we mean that our focus is on the development of the *transferable* academic study skills and language that students will need in order to be successful in a British university environment. Therefore, any content that we use is looked on as a vehicle for teaching specific skills and/or language. We are not teaching our students to pass a test, but giving them a set of tools for their toolbox that they will be able to choose from when needed in their future studies and work life.

However, we are aware that there is debate in the community about the extent to which EAP teachers need to be experts in the content and we would like to make our position on that clear here. We do not see ourselves as experts in the field of study that our students are going on to and, given that we teach differing and divergent destination groups, it is unrealistic to expect that we could ever be. This approach also fits in with some of our academic colleagues' expectations of what their roles are and what ours are. For example, the academic lead for one of our summer content-based pre-sessional courses (not IFY) as a subject expert in her field is very clear that it is her job to teach them the subject-specific content and ours to teach them the skills and language they will need to succeed. However, this should be done *through* introductory content from the students' specific degree area, which the discipline-specific academic leads choose for us to use. It is fair to say that not all academics have such a clear understanding of what it is we do and how that differs from, but yet complements, the work that they do. For those of you interested in reading more on the ESAP/EGAP debate (English for Specific/General Academic Purposes), our colleagues Bee Bond (2020) and Alex Ding (Ding and Bruce, 2017) have authored two very illuminating publications on the role of the EAP practitioner and the role of language in the wider university. Bee's book contains interviews with teachers who discuss and describe their experiences of adapting to content-based teaching, while Alex concentrates more on the wider context of EAP.

What we believe is that we need some basic knowledge in the subject area, which also naturally develops over time with familiarity with the subject, but that it is the students' job to convey information in such a way as to make the message clear to an educated but non-specialist audience. At best, then, we may think of ourselves as experts with a small 'e' in subject knowledge, but EAP teaching and assessment, in our eyes, should concentrate on the language and critical thinking skills that students need to employ in order to transmit their subject knowledge. This is our primary focus for teaching and assessment.

For us, one of the main differences between EFL teaching and EAP teaching is the way in which EAP classes should build on one another. In a typical EFL class, the language point is the teaching objective, for example, introducing different aspects of grammar as stand-alone units. Whereas, in EAP teaching, we believe it is the gradual development of specific skills and/or sub-skills that run through a series of lessons that is the key objective. For example, building note-making skills by first focusing on different strategies for making notes, giving opportunities for students to practise different ways of making notes, and then thinking about what suits them, introducing annotating as the first stage in note making, practising doing this, and then comparing their annotations with other examples, etc. So, the EFL class can be thought of as one-off, stand-alone sessions whereas EAP classes are generally not and, therefore, both teachers and students need to understand the 'bigger picture' point of doing particular activities and be reminded of how they fit into this picture.

References

Bond, B. 2020. *Making Language Visible in the University*. Bristol: Multilingual Matters.

Ding, A. and Bruce, I. 2017. *The English for Academic Purposes Practitioner: Operating on the Edge of Academia*. [Online]. [no place]: Palgrave MacMillan. [Accessed 18 March 2021]. Available from: www.vlebooks.com/Vleweb/Product/Index/1018399?page=0

Acknowledgements

The completion of this guide would not have been possible without the support of colleagues in the Language Centre at the University of Leeds, who took the time to read and comment on various draft chapters. Their expertise and guidance are gratefully acknowledged here.

Glossary of key terms and acronyms used

Advance HE: This is the new name of the former Higher Education Academy (HEA) responsible for accrediting and supporting the professional development of teaching staff in Higher Education, after the HEA's merger with the Equality Challenge Unit and the Leadership Foundation for Higher Education in 2018.
APT: Academic personal tutor.
ARC: Academic reading circles.
BALEAP: The British Association of Lecturers in English for Academic Purposes. There is an organisation in the UK, which you may have heard of, called BALEAP. They play a pivotal role in setting and maintaining the standards in EAP in the HE sector and they accredit courses run in UK universities. You can read more on the BALEAP website www.baleap.org/ and, by the way, this can be a useful resource for jobs too since many UK universities advertise their posts through BALEAP.
BC: The British Council. This is an international organisation that acts as an accreditation body as well as running teacher training courses and English language schools, and offering examinations such as IELTS. Since they are globally known, having your language school provision approved and accredited through them can be beneficial to its reputation and it is also another place you might find employment opportunities. They also have a magazine with teaching tips. For more information about any of the things they do, check out their website: www.britishcouncil.org/.
CA: Constructive alignment. This is a term first coined by Biggs in the 90s. For making sure that learning outcomes, all course input, teaching, and assessment match so that what is taught is what is assessed and vice versa. Assessments should assess all the intended learning outcomes without over assessment.

Glossary of key terms and acronyms used xi

EAP: The teaching of English for Academic Purposes. We will use the acronym EAP to refer to the teaching of English for Academic Purposes, although there is a distinction made between **ESAP** (English for *Specific* Academic Purposes) and **EGAP** (English for *General* Academic Purposes). ESAP is where the cohort is from the same discipline area and the content and assessments can, therefore, be tailored specifically to that discipline area. EGAP is more suited for mixed discipline cohorts with content and assessments that are necessarily more generic. There is some debate between academics as to which of these is a better pedagogic choice but, since this depends a lot on your context, we will simply refer to both types of teaching in this guide as EAP.

EFL: The teaching of English as a Foreign Language. For the purposes of this guide, any type of language teaching other than for academic purposes will be referred to as **EFL**. Other types of teaching of this kind are **ESL** (English as a *Second* Language), **ESOL** (English to Speakers of *Other* Languages), and even **EMI** (English as a *Medium* of *Instruction*), where different subjects are taught in English.

HE: Higher Education (university) as opposed to **FE**, which is Further Education (college), but both are post compulsory school study.

IELTS: International English Language Testing System. These are tests accepted for university entry worldwide.

IFY: International Foundation Year. Again, there may be various acronyms for this such as **IFP** (where P is for Programme), but we will use IFY to refer to any foundational course. In fact, using the word 'year' is a little misleading since most university foundation courses run for nine months or less of an academic year.

LO: Learning outcomes. These are the desired or intended goals for students studying on a particular module. These are sometimes referred to as **ILO**s.

NHS: The UK's National Health Service.

PPP: Presentation-Practice-Production. This is a 3 phase framework used to teach grammar and vocabulary structures. It moves from presentation of the grammar point/vocabulary items through to tightly controlled practice, ending with more relaxed and meaningful experimentation.

Recycling: This refers to the building in of repeated opportunities for students to practise a skill or competency. For example, the mechanics of referencing need to be brought into different materials in different ways so that students become more

	familiar with the requirements and to allow them to develop their accuracy. This will include features of compiling a reference list and in-text citations and may include putting sources into alphabetical order (for Harvard style referencing), using capital letters, commas, full stops, italics, bold, and brackets appropriately in reference lists. When to include speech marks and page numbers, how to cite original authors in other authors' work, distinguishing between different texts written by the same author in the same year are some of the features of in-text citations students will need to know.
Scaffolding:	This refers to support that you may need to build in to assist students in getting from point A to point B. If you wish to run a marathon, let's say, you might start by running 100 metres and building up to the whole race in increments. It is the same idea with learning. Students can't necessarily get all the way from point A to point B without some interim steps, guidance, and input to help them get there. As students progress through their course, scaffolding can gradually be reduced and removed as independence gradually increases.
Syllabus:	We use the term 'syllabus' in this guide to refer to a programme or course. What we mean by syllabus is the creation of a coherent series of sessions that incorporate the relevant academic skills and language to address the needs of the students in preparation for their future study.
TBL:	Task-based learning. This approach begins with students attempting a language task with minimal instruction and is split into a 3 stage framework: pre-task, task cycle and language focus. It begins with students experimenting and negotiating with each other to complete the task, and ends with controlled practice. It is the opposite of PPP.
Tutor/teacher:	You will see that we have used both of these terms in this guide. They should be viewed as being interchangeable, but we mean the person leading classroom sessions (whether this is online or face to face). When we refer to **personal tutoring**, we mean an academic teacher/tutor assigned to a group of students for discussions about the students' educational progress.
UG:	Undergraduate a student's first degree studies.
UKAT:	The United Kingdom Advising and Tutoring Association, which is responsible for all aspects of student advising and personal tutoring in UK Higher Education.
VLE:	Virtual Learning Environment.
Washback:	The washback effect refers to the effect of assessment on the teaching/learning process. In other words, learning is built from assessment and washed back into the classroom.

An introduction to this guide

Who is this guide aimed at?

EAP is still in its infancy in relative terms, but there are an increasing number of books available on the market. As with any 'new' or 'young' discipline, it is clearly important for it to establish its credibility in order for it to be taken seriously by others, and of course it is necessary to underpin practice with relevant theory and research. However, we feel that busy teachers, particularly those who are new to EAP, might need something more practical to begin with. Therefore, this guide is very much aimed at the novice EAP teacher. 'Novice' in this context is a relative term since both of us came to EAP teaching with some experience of doing it in some form already and with a lot of English to Speakers of Other Languages (ESOL) teaching experience, but most of what we know now we learned on the job. You may also be an EAP practitioner already, but, for you, IFY teaching might be a new experience. Or it might be that you are new to some aspect of its management, course design, or materials writing. You may be working in an international context in isolation and/or without ready access to resources. So, rather than look at one or two aspects of IFY teaching, this guide aims to cover all elements of IFY course design, management, and materials for a beginner-level practitioner with the hope that it tells you at least some of the things we wish we had known right from the beginning of our IFY journey.

Although there are a number of publications that focus on EAP, none deal exclusively with IFY teaching. We feel that it merits looking at in its own right because of its unique position as a bridge between school and university life. However, not everything about teaching IFY is different. It is still EAP teaching, so some aspects are more generic than others.

It is also important to keep in mind that, although we are writing from our own experience, which is in a UK university context, we are aware that there are many foundation courses around the world that do not operate in exactly the same way and may well not be run according to UK policies and procedures. It is for this reason that we are not going to tie the content too closely to all 'hot topics' on the agenda in HE institutions in this country. For example, initiatives such as the 'compassionate curriculum' or 'decolonising the curriculum' and other current trends may or may not be as relevant to your particular context as they are to ours, nor will the focus of attention remain static over time. So, while we may touch on inclusivity and diversity issues as an important element of working with *individuals* within a group, we will not dwell on the details of university policy or UK law. That is not to say that mental health and well-being are not important or that we shouldn't be looking to find ways of building these things into our teaching pedagogy and into the curricula in a compassionate way, but that these things may be at different stages in different countries or indeed within different institutions. It is, therefore, up to the individual reading this guide to decide what merits further exploration and when.

However, the basic premise guiding all our provision in the Language Centre (not just our IFY provision) is to choose content, tasks, and topics that include and enable *all* members of a cohort to contribute as equitably as possible, which encompasses both inclusivity and decolonising the curriculum.

What underpins this guide

With all of this in mind, this guide focuses more on the practical aspects of delivering an IFY course and is therefore a much lighter touch on theory. The assumption being that, once you gain confidence and experience, you can then go on to read any number of the very good publications already on the market to dig deeper into the theory behind what you do and to question things further.

The role of BALEAP in this guide

As BALEAP plays such a pivotal role in setting and maintaining the standards in EAP in the UK university sector, we have taken the BALEAP (2008) Competency Framework for Teachers of English for Academic Purposes (otherwise known as TEAP) to underpin our guide. This framework focuses very much on teaching and so it makes sense to us that *everyone* teaching EAP, whether in a university or not, whether in the UK or abroad, follows the same framework to underpin their teaching in order to develop a shared understanding of what it is that we do, and ultimately to aim for greater consistency in the field in a global context.

The assumption we have made is that the majority of students wish to come to the UK in order to complete their degree or to attend an establishment in their own country that has a UK base or partnership. Clearly, even if this assumption were always to be true, there may still be elements of the TEAP competency framework that are not applicable in certain circumstances (e.g., teacher knowledge of a particular policy at a specific university). These may be things for the students themselves to find out about at a later date. However, this doesn't necessarily mean that the IFY teacher shouldn't have a generic understanding of UK university policies and procedures. The

An introduction to this guide xv

competency area is 'competencies relating to academic practice' and is further categorised as 'Academic Contexts' (BALEAP, 2008, p4). The descriptor for this competency is worded as 'the EAP teacher will have *a reasonable knowledge* of the organizational, educational, and communicative policies, practices, values and conventions of universities' (BALEAP, 2008, p4). It is therefore the responsibility of the individual to determine what *reasonable* knowledge is within their own specific context.

Since we began writing this guide, BALEAP have announced that the framework is undergoing a review. We don't have access to the details of changes to the framework at this time because the updated version is only due to come out in 2022. However, what we do know is that the pedagogy of teaching EAP is not going to change. What is being taken into consideration by BALEAP is the international applicability of the competencies. The framework was originally written for a UK context, but condensing the existing framework competencies should make it more relevant to differing contexts outside the UK. Therefore, we have no hesitation in keeping the 2008 competencies as our guiding principles.

How to use this guide

It is our assumption that you will not read this book from cover to cover, but rather dip in and out of it as and when you need to. Each chapter should be thought of as a section in a ring binder which you would turn to as appropriate for your current needs. Therefore, you may notice some overlap in content where certain aspects are discussed in relation to the particular perspective of the chapter. So, for example, plagiarism is discussed in both Chapter 1 and 5.

At the start of each chapter, first you will see the BALEAP competencies we think are the most relevant, next you will find a short chapter summary, and, at the end of each chapter, there are some reflection questions. If you are working as part of a team, these can be discussion questions but, clearly, if you are working alone, you can still derive some benefit from being a reflective practitioner.

Although this is a guide rather than a coursebook, we have included a few example materials in some chapters. This is in order to illustrate the points we are trying to make. You may wish to adapt or adopt some of these ideas to suit your own teaching context, but, otherwise, just treat them as visual aids.

Reference

BALEAP. 2008. *Competency Framework for Teachers of English for Academic Purposes*. [Online]. [Accessed 16 January 2019]. Available from: www.baleap.org/wp-content/uploads/2016/04/teap-competency-framework.pdf

1 The challenges of academic culture

Relevant BALEAP competencies:

Academic contexts:
1. *An EAP teacher will have a reasonable knowledge of the organizational, educational and communicative policies, practices, values and conventions of universities.*

Student needs:
5. *An EAP teacher will understand the requirements of the target context that students wish to enter as well as the needs of students in relation to their prior learning experiences and how these might influence their current educational expectations.*

(BALEAP, 2008)

Student expectations

There may be all kinds of resistance to change for foundation year students on leaving high school and moving into Higher Education (HE), and this can range from a student finding it difficult to move from the more narrative style of writing they have been used to at school to a more formal, academic style, to a student sleeping in class as this is acceptable in a culture where long classes require them to take a power nap from time to time. These issues should be raised and discussed, where appropriate, and can lead to some interesting discussions on how educational culture and behaviour vary in different types of contexts.

The BALEAP competencies above outline the importance of tutors being familiar with the norms and conventions of their educational institution in relation to teaching and learning, staff/student communication and assessment, and of being familiar with ethical practices, respect for intellectual property, disciplinary procedures, and student support. If a member of staff is new to the institution, time will need to be spent familiarising them with how systems work so that they are able to pass on this information confidently to their students.

DOI: 10.4324/9781003253624-1

2 The challenges of academic culture

From the very first week of the course, it is vital that student expectations are discussed, so that they are fully aware of what is required of them and what they should in turn expect of staff and the institution. This is a time to encourage conversations around students' previous learning experiences and educational environments and how this may differ to the one they are now part of. Foundation year students, particularly those who may be moving to a new country to study, may find the acculturation process quite brutal in the first few weeks. Most of them are having to negotiate living alone for the first time in a new country and all that that entails (shopping, cooking, laundering clothes, getting out of bed and going places to a strict schedule) and, at the same time, are finding themselves inside a system of education that may not make sense to them on many levels.

There needs to be some flexibility in the first couple of weeks of the first semester regarding students coming to class late, not checking timetables, not reading emails, and so on. However, students must be told firmly that this cannot continue and will have a detrimental impact on their academic development and the way in which they are perceived by tutors if this becomes habitual. The consequences should be explained so they are aware that consistent lateness or attitude problems will be passed on to the programme head and disciplinary steps will be taken if necessary. For example, if students are sponsored, then sponsors will be informed. It very rarely reaches this stage and the first personal tutorial can be used productively to find out why students are struggling with timekeeping, etc., and solutions discussed. The details of disciplinary procedures should be transparent and stored in a place where students can have easy access to them, preferably on the module VLE page.

Communication

Communicating with tutors/academic staff

Most tutors may have a relaxed, friendly teaching style, which may give students the impression that they can 'formally' communicate with them, by email, for example, or anyone else in the same casual, informal way they would with friends, sending emails littered with emojis and exclamation marks, or, as second language users, they may inadvertently use language that sounds demanding and rude. Neither of these approaches will get the best response from the recipient. While you may not have a problem with being addressed by your first name, for example, and may have told your students to address you in this way, not all tutors institution-wide will feel the same and we would be doing students a great disservice by not explaining how the system of address works in the academic culture they find themselves in or may find themselves in in the future. Input on communication could be included in the induction programme activities, for example, at Leeds we include it as part of a general 'introduction to life at a British university' session for our international students and, rather than laying down the rules, set up a discussion around this with questions such as: 'How did you address your teacher at school?' 'Would it be appropriate to address your lecturer in the same way?' Below is a typical activity we use along with some (optional) useful phrases, although, depending on the language level of your class, you may prefer students to generate their own. The topic is 'politeness'. Not to suggest that non-UK students are not polite, but just that there are culturally bound ways of expressing it. The worksheet below includes examples of face-to-face communication between tutors and students and lends itself to a possible role-playing activity.

Covid-19 and teaching online

It is necessary to add a codicil to the above since the pandemic, as the subsequent move to teaching online has prompted an unforeseen shift in the way in which we communicate with colleagues and students. The use of platforms such as Microsoft Teams often means that you may receive a '♥' response to an announcement such as 'Please ensure that all essay drafts are submitted through Turnitin by 9am, UK time', which can be disconcerting, but at the same time it seems churlish to tell students that this is not acceptable (in fact, a heart emoji can give an exhausted tutor a much-needed boost, to be honest). I have been guilty of just letting this be after a very long day of being glued to a screen. In the great scheme of things, it's not such an issue as long as students are polite and respectful to tutors and each other, and that they are aware that email communication with a tutor they do not know still needs to adhere to the appropriate, more formal, conventions. However, as it now seems that online teaching is going to be with us for some time to come, if not for good, then we should be discussing how this is going to impact on our teaching and delivery, particularly with regard to the etiquette we expect from students in the virtual classroom. Do we, for example, expect students to have their cameras switched on throughout the session? How do we want students to engage in discussion when it is not so easy to read body language? How are we going to promote a supportive and engaging learning environment when we are effectively losing the spontaneous learning opportunities we had in the classroom?

Below is a worksheet we have used with our students in a face-to-face teaching scenario, which usually sparks off interesting discussions around politeness and etiquette.

Politeness

Task 1

Discuss the following questions in small groups of mixed nationalities (if possible):

How do people in your country show politeness?
How have you observed that people in England show politeness?

Task 2

Look at the following situations. In pairs, discuss what you would say and write down any useful phrases that you could use.

a   You arrive late for a lesson and want to explain why to your tutor.
b   You go to your tutor's office to ask for some help with an assignment. Your tutor is busy.
c   You go to your tutor's office to ask for some help with an assignment. Your tutor is not there, but another member of staff is.
d   You don't agree with what your tutor is advising you to do in a tutorial.
e   You don't agree with something your tutor says in a lesson.
f   You are looking for a tutor. You find two members of staff in the middle of a conversation. You want to ask them.

Task 3

Compare the phrases you wrote down with the list of phrases your tutor gives you. See if there are any that you missed. Or, are there any you can add to the list?

Task 4

Now practise using the phrases in groups of three. You need one student, one tutor, and one observer in each group. Spend a few minutes role playing each of the six scenarios from Task 2. The observer's job is to comment on how polite the student and the tutor were to one another. Change roles so that everyone has the opportunity to be the student, the tutor, and the observer.

Task 5

Together in your group of three, discuss why it is important to think about politeness in a university context:

- 1...
- 2...
- 3...

Useful phrases

Excuse me...
I'm sorry to disturb you.
I'm sorry to interrupt.

> Please could you help me?
> Have you got a moment?
> Would you mind telling me where (Mr / Miss / Mrs / Dr / Professor) …….. is?
> Please could you tell me where (Mr / Miss / Mrs / Dr / Professor) …….. is?
> I'd like to apologise for………
> Can / May I explain why I ………..?
> I'm not sure about that. I think ……
> Actually, I think it's better to ………
> I think there may be another possibility / answer.
> Would it be possible to ……?
> Is it also right to say … .?
> Thank you very / so much (for your help / advice).

Inter-personal skills

Good inter-personal skills are required in most of the students' target contexts, and these range from being able to work successfully in a group to offering support and encouragement to each other throughout the year.

The age of the students and the lack of life experience has to be considered, which may mean that some 'training' is needed so that they are able to work productively together, accept and give constructive criticism, and respect and support each other even if opinions on certain things differ. As a first step in this conversation, all students should be made aware of their institution's policy on *'dignity and mutual respect'*, if there is one, and that various behaviours such as victimisation, bullying, and harassment are not tolerated within or outside the classroom and action will be taken. Discussions on this can be included in induction week. If students are at an institution that does not have these types of policies, there can still be conversations around mutual respect as a way of preparing them for the next stage of their studies.

IFY classes can either be mono-cultural or there could a whole mix of nationalities in one class, either way students need to understand that, for the rest of their academic career, they will meet and work with other students who have had a very different life experience to them and may hold opinions that they do not agree with, which they need to respond to in a respectful manner. It may also be useful to have discussions around the local culture they now find themselves in if you are teaching an international cohort; students will become more and more aware of differences as they settle in and may ask tutors questions about this. Leeds, as an example, is a city with a vibrant nightlife, which tends to involve alcohol; this is very evident on a Friday and Saturday night when the streets in the city centre are packed with some very inebriated people, which may be a shock for students who come from cultures where alcohol does not play a key role in socialising, or may be banned. Conversations around these situations should be very much encouraged and often are the start of deeper mutual understanding of each other's cultures.

IFY students will be expected to learn how to work with, and relate to, each other in group scenarios and this is something that should be part of a study skills module so that they feel comfortable working in groups and can understand the inherent pitfalls. Most degree programmes include groupwork in their suite of assessments and so preparation for this is essential. Part of class time should involve informal discussion in groups, which is monitored by the tutor, so that students see this as a natural part of higher education. Seminars are part of the education process for the majority of undergraduate programmes and there should be opportunities to analyse previous groups' videos for examples of useful language and technique and opportunities to practice throughout the year in the relatively 'safe' environment of the study skills classroom. Discussing and practising ways of dealing with what could go wrong, such as becoming tongue-tied, sounding nervous, or not being able to answer questions will help students to create a bank of useful strategies for the future. Most importantly, it helps build resistance to criticism. Because of the young age of our students and their general lack of life experience, many of them see criticism as a negative experience and participating in a seminar discussion provides the ideal environment for constructive criticism, where students can train in ways of giving and accepting useful comments that are meant to aid development. Having a seminar discussion as an assessment is a good way to enforce how important a part of undergraduate study these skills are.

Criticality and unconscious bias

Critical thinking will be raised throughout this book because it is considered a key skill for IFY students embarking on the first steps of their academic journey. As we often tell them, good critical thinking is not some unattainable goal far off in the future, they already do it in their everyday lives. In fact, an effective way to open the discussion on critical thinking is to ask students why they chose their current university over others? What were the criteria they used? Was it success rates? Employment prospects? Good campus life? Near to good transport links? Who or what did they consult? Current students? The prospectus? The media? Who do they trust the most? Why? When you pose critical thinking in this way, it is easy for students to understand that they already have the necessary skills to evaluate and analyse, but they now need to consider applying them to academic work.

The greatest hurdle for foundation students is not that they cannot think critically, but that they are young, mostly with little life experience, and they often lack confidence. If they come from a culture where teachers are revered, they may initially be reluctant to disagree with or challenge the opinions of tutors or the opinions found in journal articles. However, work on evaluating sources, understanding bias, and determining what constitutes sound evidence will help to raise awareness and build confidence in this area.

As well as being aware of how bias can relate to academic work, there is also a need for students to understand how it applies it to their everyday interactions and relationships with their tutors, their peers, and essentially anyone they encounter both within and outside their educational institution. We all harbour unconscious biases towards others, and the significant impact of this on many aspects of academic life has come to the fore in recent years and HE institutions have begun offering workshops for staff on the topic of unconscious or implicit bias. After attending a couple of these staff sessions, I contacted the academic responsible for them and we discussed the possibility of using similar material with students as an awareness-raising activity. Our current cohort at Leeds are all moving into the field of healthcare as medics, dentists, nurses, and audiologists, and will be meeting patients and colleagues from various walks of life, so it seemed logical to discuss this issue with them as part of discussions around ethical practice. Healthcare profession codes of practice all refer to treating patients with dignity and respect, for example, the **Nursing and Midwifery Council** specify the following in their professional code of practice:

---

1 Treat people as individuals and uphold their dignity

To achieve this, you must:

1.1 treat people with kindness, respect and compassion
1.2 make sure you deliver the fundamentals of care effectively
1.3 avoid making assumptions and recognise diversity and individual choice
1.4 make sure that any treatment, assistance or care for which you are responsible is delivered without undue delay
1.5 respect and uphold people's human rights

(The Nursing and Midwifery Council, 2018, p6)

Point 1.3 is particularly relevant. Students coming to Leeds, or indeed the UK, for the first time may be surprised, or even shocked, by the diversity of its inhabitants in terms of ethnicity, religion, sexuality, lifestyle choices, and so on, if this is something they are not used to. As healthcare professionals, they may meet patients whose health issues are a product of their lifestyle, for example, liver failure in an alcoholic patient, and judgements may be made about the patient based on their own values. Therefore, some unconscious bias training is needed so that they are aware of where their biases lie and so that they do not negatively affect the relationships they have with patients and colleagues. On the flipside, some of our international students may have been at the receiving end of someone else's biases and so it is important for them to recognise this, to know that it is not acceptable, and that they have a right to report it or confront it.

It was easy to feed this into the syllabus on the *Academic Study Skills for Dentistry, Medicine, and Healthcare Professions* module because the first 'project' covered in semester 1 is **Ethics in Healthcare**, so it is a natural follow-on from discussions surrounding medical ethics and professionalism. It also connects very well with induction materials, as unconscious bias can be related to our university policy on dignity and mutual respect. The University of Leeds is now trying to make unconscious bias part of the induction package for all students in the same way that academic integrity is. While this is welcome, I would argue that the most effective way for it to be introduced would be by the module tutor, in small tutor groups, where it could be linked to degree subjects in some way and in small groups students might feel more comfortable discussing their own biases with others.

We covered this topic in one two-hour session and followed these three basic steps:

Step 1

Give students a 'dilemma' to consider, a good example to use is one known as the 'The Father Son Activity' or 'The Surgeon's Dilemma':

> *A father and son were involved in a car accident in which the father was killed and the son was seriously injured. The father was pronounced dead at the scene of the accident and his body was taken to a local morgue. The son was taken by ambulance to a nearby hospital and was immediately wheeled into an emergency operating room. A surgeon was called. Upon arrival and seeing the patient, the attending surgeon exclaimed "Oh my God, it's my son!" Can you explain this?*
>
> (Culture Plus Consulting, 2018)

This opens up the topic of unconscious bias as you discuss the reasons why you may have given a particular response to this dilemma. It is an example of gender bias and students could be asked to discuss what other types of bias they are aware of, prompting answers such as bias based on religion, ethnicity, sexual orientation, age, disability, and so on, essentially listing the protected characteristics that are enshrined in UK Equality Law.

This can be followed by another activity known as the 'Circle of Trust' (Culture Plus Consulting, 2018), whereby students are asked to list 6–10 people they know and trust, excluding family members. The tutor then reads out some of the protected characteristics, for example, gender, religion, ethnicity, age, and so on, and students tick the people on their list who most resemble them in this characteristic. When asked to consider their lists, they will probably find that most, if not all, of the people on it resemble them. Known as 'affinity bias', this is the point where students can be prompted to discuss some of the general everyday implications of this.

Step 2

The following TED talk allows for some practice of listening for gist and further opportunities to discuss what unconscious bias means:

> TEDx Talks. 2013. Inclusion, Exclusion, Illusion and Collusion. [Online]. [Accessed 20 August 2019]. Available from: Inclusion, Exclusion, Illusion and Collusion: Helen Turnbull at TEDxDelrayBeach – YouTube

Step 3

If students are in any doubt as to the impact of unconscious bias, show the following statistics. Some of these are particularly relevant to healthcare and can prompt further discussion about the implications of unconscious bias in healthcare settings.

In the UK
Equality and Human Rights Commission Report, August 2016 (EHRC, 2016):
- Black people are treated more harshly in the criminal justice system. You are more than three times more likely to be prosecuted and sentenced if you are Black than if you are White.
- Black workers with degrees earn 23.1% less on average than White workers with equivalent degrees.
- In Britain, significantly lower percentages of ethnic minorities (8.8%) work as managers, directors, and senior officials, compared with White people (10.7%).
- Black people who leave school with A-levels typically get paid 14.3% less than their White peers.
- Black African women have a mortality rate four times higher than White women in the UK
- Black African women are seven times more likely to be detained under mental health legislation in England and Wales than White British women.

*I am grateful to Dr Tasia Scrutton (School of Philosophy, Religion, and History of Science, University of Leeds) for granting permission to use some of her slides (the above being one of them) from her staff workshop.

What is vital in this session is that students are assured that they will not be judged negatively on their views/opinions. If this session is to be successful, participants must feel that they can discuss situations where they may have held bias and how they might react differently next time. It may be beneficial to explain how awareness of unconscious bias is part of the personal criticality and reflection required in academia.

Academic integrity

One area of study that is, arguably, the most important for any student in HE is that of academic integrity, but do international students require more support with this than home students? This quote from the Higher Education Academy (HEA) publication 'Addressing Plagiarism' summarises very well the challenge for international students:

> *The Australian IDP research database on international education lists more than 100 papers on this issue, most of which agree that unintentional plagiarism is due to students either assuming the expectations have not changed from previous writing contexts and/ or they do not understand how to apply the UK rules, once they are aware of them.*
>
> (HEA, 2014, p4)

Pecorari (2003) supports this by citing anecdotal cases of international students producing work that, although lacking in sufficient attribution, was not intentional plagiarism and was due perhaps to the way in which students' own cultures approach the use of others' works in writing. They display a tendency towards what would certainly be labelled 'academic malpractice', and this is, often, unintentional. Unfortunately, the rules regarding academic malpractice in HE establishments do not distinguish between intentional or unintentional plagiarism when imposing penalties, thus highlighting the real need for students to be aware of what is expected of them in terms of academic integrity.

The main reasons for IFY students committing academic malpractice in our experience are:

1   Coming from a cultural background where copying someone's work is seen as a sign of respect.
2   Coming from a culture where rote-learning is common. Most of our students come straight from high school where this might have been the prescribed method of preparation for exams. Not all students have experience of essay-writing as a form of continuous assessment.
3   Not fully understanding the principles behind referencing.
4   Being worried about language proficiency and making mistakes when writing or not feeling they can paraphrase well enough.

5   Struggling with time management and feeling overwhelmed with work and the pressure to perform, so much so that a student resorts to copying and pasting or does not have the time to paraphrase well.
6   Panic – we have noted that, if there are any cases of plagiarism/malpractice, they are more likely to occur in semester 2 if semester 1 grades were not reaching the required target for progression.

The above are the most common reasons, and of course there will be a minority of students who wilfully commit malpractice by commissioning essays through essay mills or who copy from each other or from students from previous years who may have submitted a similar assignment. However, in our experience, these students are very rare. Our stance on plagiarism and malpractice is that students do not want to cheat but need continuous guidance during their foundation year on how to avoid doing this unintentionally.

How to help students understand the importance of academic integrity and avoid malpractice

The 2014 HEA guide 'Addressing Plagiarism' suggests that *'solutions are best addressed at different levels of authority and responsibility'* (p5). An institution's academic integrity officer, foundation year programme lead, or study skills module leader can often provide the institution's stance on plagiarism and malpractice in a live introductory lecture. A lecture such as this, which often covers the penalties meted out for the various degrees of malpractice, can initially frighten students; this is where the class tutor and personal tutor step in and lead the discussion on understanding plagiarism and strategies to avoid it at a more informal level.

Step 1: Begin semester 1 with a live lecture by one of your institution's *'academic integrity officers'*. If that is not possible because your institution doesn't have anyone in this role, then by the module/programme leader. This comes from a position of real authority, essentially the institution's view on plagiarism and the way to deal with it, which can be daunting to new students. Ideally, this should be done in conjunction with a class session by the tutor on the definition of plagiarism and a brief introduction to methods of referencing and citing sources.

Step 2: Provide opportunities in class with class tutor for students to practise the 'mechanics' of citing and referencing. Provide opportunities for questions regarding the academic integrity lecture. Have discussions around how it might be possible to avoid plagiarism and malpractice. So, having heard the institution's position on academic integrity in **step 1**, the tutor can step in as another 'authority', but one that is slightly more benign and in a position to provide support.

Step 3: Introduce Turnitin, the software that checks for similarity between student work and online sources. This is an essential tool for staff, but students need to know how to use it (see lesson plan below). Allowing students to see their own Turnitin reports after submitting a piece of work is often when the theory begins to make sense to them.

Step 4: Give continuous guidance throughout the year. Teaching materials should allow for opportunities to annotate texts and note-take in a way that helps students to see annotating and note-taking as anti-plagiarism tools. Analyse good/bad examples of paraphrasing, show examples of *good through to excellent* past student work. If all the examples are L1 speaker models, then they can appear impossible to emulate, so show work from across the spectrum. Allow time to discuss how we use writers' work in our own to build up an argument; students often struggle to understand how to create their own voice in their work when it seems we are asking them to simply quote and paraphrase the experts.

Using Turnitin as a teaching tool

Alongside the conversation you have with your students regarding academic integrity, you should also introduce them to Turnitin so that they understand how it operates and are able to navigate their own similarity reports if they are given an opportunity to do so. We suggest that students are allowed to see the Turnitin reports for their formative work and that this is used as a learning opportunity by identifying poor paraphrasing, for example. It is important for them to know that it isn't a 'plagiarism detector', but rather a tool that detects similarity between student work and online sources. Tutors must check all areas highlighted as similar very carefully as they may be legitimate, for example, a quotation that has used quotation marks and has been cited correctly. Below is part of a lesson where Turnitin is introduced to students (N.B. not all the documents have been included in this lesson plan, it is just an example of the kind of lesson you could create to raise awareness of what Turnitin does):

Lesson plan

The **aim** of the lesson is:

- to understand what 'Turnitin' is and how to 'read' a Turnitin report.

Turnitin

Turnitin is used by most UK universities, including Leeds, and is a text-matching service. When a piece of work is submitted to Turnitin, it generates a Turnitin *Originality Report* by comparing the submitted piece of work with sources from the internet. It highlights where there is a similarity between the submitted paper and this internet database. It will give a similarity percentage. Turnitin is not a 'plagiarism index', but a 'similarity index', which means that the tutor has to check the report carefully to see if the similarity is genuine or if the student has plagiarised. Figure 1.1 is an example of a page from a student's originality report:

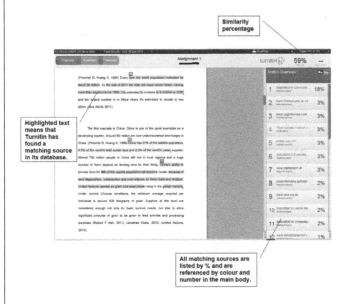

Figure 1.1 Sample Turnitin similarity report.

Task 1

Your tutor will give you three pages from a student's Turnitin report so that you can try and explain the similarity and decide if the student has plagiarised, or if there is another reason for the similarity.

Work with a partner:

1 Look at the first example in red. Is this plagiarism? Why/why not?
2 Look at the second and third examples in red. Is this plagiarism? Why/why not?
3 Look at the *'match overview'* for the examples in red. It reads 'Submitted to University of Leeds'. Why do you think this is the case with those three examples?
4 Look at section 2, example 14. Is this plagiarism? Why/why not?
5 Try and paraphrase example 14.
6 In section 2, are there any problems with examples 13 and 17?
7 Look at section 3, examples 6 and 2. What advice would you give the student to improve this section?

What do you think are some of the limitations of using Turnitin?

N.B. Turnitin also checks similarity with other pieces of work that students have submitted both at the University of Leeds and other universities. Therefore, if you collude with another student on IFY or copy chunks from the work of a previous student, this will be very apparent to your tutor. Changing one or two words in an attempt to make this less obvious is never successful. In these cases, **both students will be penalised**, the student who has copied and the student who has been copied from.

The family connection

Often on IFY programmes, students will have siblings or cousins who have passed through the programme before them and, if a student is feeling under pressure to finish assignments, there could be a temptation to seek help from them.

It is beneficial to explain to your class that this is never advisable and that all former essays are stored on Turnitin and therefore it is not a wise move to use any parts of another student's work. If the module has a set assignment that requires students to choose their own aspect of a topic, then it may be a good idea in the early planning stages to check that your students have not been tempted to seek help in this way and, if they have, then this would be the right time to have a conversation with them before submission and when they still have plenty of time to rethink and rewrite the assignment task. This is only possible if you know that a student has a sibling who has been on the programme and if the current student's work either **a)** appears familiar and on checking clearly is not the student's own work or **b)** is too sophisticated for this particular student. Intervening in this way before a student submits work is one of the most impactful ways for a student to understand the rules surrounding academic integrity. It signals to the student that you care about their academic development and that it is possible for tutors to recognise the signs of malpractice (intentional or otherwise) without the help of Turnitin. The earlier you can intervene in academic integrity issues with foundation year students the better. Foundation year is a formative year and students are finding their way around the system and need support. However, it needs to be an *'iron fist in a kid glove approach'* because, at the same time, students need to understand the gravity of plagiarism and the impact it can have on their studies.

We have never subscribed to the view that assessments should be changed every year so that students are not tempted to plagiarise a previous student's work. This often means changes to course input and is not always practical for module leaders/materials writers who might not have time to implement all the necessary changes. Ultimately, we have to trust that the majority of students understand the implications of academic malpractice and are given the support they need during the writing process.

Penalties for academic malpractice

The question that most students ask during conversations on plagiarism is '*what will happen if I plagiarise?*' and there is no straightforward answer to this. In a university scenario, at the very worst expulsion through to re-writing the piece of work and receiving a capped mark to losing a few marks because a few sentences have been poorly paraphrased. It is very unlikely that an IFY student would be expelled for a first offence and nor should they be if foundation year is to do what it says on the tin, which is to support students in their transition to academic life. Tutors should never play down plagiarism though, and IFY students should never be under the impression that they will be dealt with lightly just because they are on an essentially 'formative' programme. Module leaders should ensure that students are able to access, and are familiar with, their institution's policy on academic integrity and that they can see for themselves the possible penalties.

When beginning to introduce the topic of academic integrity to students there must be a fine balance between ensuring that they understand the severity of plagiarism for their academic futures and not frightening them so much that they daren't put pen to paper. The fear of being 'convicted' is often overwhelming and the question students ask the most during writing consultations is 'What if I've accidentally plagiarised?' Cottrell (2001) raises an important point regarding the complexity of the concept of plagiarism for some of our students. They may have difficulty understanding where groupwork ends and individual work begins, they may have trouble knowing what we mean when we ask for original pieces of work, especially when everything has to be supported by the work of experts. Cottrell (2001) cites examples of students looking at academic journal articles and seeing that all academics seem to do is to quote each other with very little original input; this can be confusing and the concept of 'voice' in writing is one that can be introduced as part of conversations on this.

The best way to deal with all of the above is a step-by-step approach. Rest assured there will be many questions from students, usually fuelled by anxiety, and the best course of action as a module leader/materials writer/tutor is to try and ensure that the module slowly introduces what is needed at the right time. Any opportunities to exploit academic texts and/or student sample work for the purpose of furthering student understanding of this complex issue is welcome.

Understanding the needs of the target context

Module leaders and materials writers for IFY study skills modules should always begin with an exploration of the students' target context/s before beginning to design a syllabus (see Chapter 2 for more detailed focus on this). Students should also be informed about their target context, and this will mean allowing time in class for students to access university programme catalogues for details of their future degree programme. Direct them to course information, particularly course content and structure, learning and teaching methods, assessment types, and reading lists. Conversations around the skills required for the various assessment types and the amount of reading they are expected to do should help students to understand the value of study skills.

The value of subject-specific content

Most foundation year courses involve students following the typical subjects required for entry to their designated degree programme, usually with a study skills module added as support with the necessary writing, reading, listening and speaking skills. For example, in our context at Leeds, a student hoping to study Medicine would take maths, chemistry, and biology in addition to study skills and would need specific grades to be accepted.

Study skills are very rarely taught in isolation, and I would go as far as to say they shouldn't be and that projects or specific topics should be utilised as a vehicle for these skills. If you are in the fortunate position of teaching a group of students who will be studying similar degree programmes, such as Engineering students or students moving into Healthcare, then there are possibilities for context-based preparation that reflects their future discipline not only in the required skills, but also in terms of content. The ideal situation for any foundation year module leader/designer, if part of a university, is to have strong ties with the students' receiving departments and to be able to follow the '*cooperation, collaboration, team-teaching*' method advocated by Dudley-Evans and St John (1998). This is not always possible for many reasons, if university departments are only receiving a handful of IFY students they may not feel like dedicating much time to this and the most you can expect is an email with some links to useful coursebooks/journal articles, which can be mined for useful subject-specific language. Others may be keen, offering to deliver basic lectures on some of the content, even going as far as team-teaching, sitting in on assessments, and becoming involved with grading, but this is the ideal rather than the norm.

Using content from students' future disciplines benefits student motivation in a module that can give the impression of being a bit 'dry'. We can forgive 17–18-year-olds for not being inspired by the idea of study skills, but teaching skills within projects that are stimulating goes a long way to turning it into a module they enjoy attending. The Leeds IFY Study Skills for Dentistry, Medicine, and Healthcare module uses the following four healthcare-based projects throughout the year:

SEMESTER 1	*Ethics in Healthcare*
	The NHS Crisis
SEMESTER 2	*Health Promotion*
	Issues in Healthcare

These were chosen after discussions with lecturers from the Schools of Dentistry, Medicine, and Nursing. The 'NHS Crisis' project is particularly welcomed by receiving departments as all of the students on the module have to train within the NHS system and need to understand how it operates and what to expect, and they would be significantly disadvantaged if they did not possess knowledge of the healthcare system in which they will be training. Although IFY healthcare students are not allowed onto hospital wards for any clinical training, watching the recent BBC Hospital series, for example, provides a good enough substitute. Students are often asked to watch an episode at home from a particular perspective, take notes, and then share what they learned with their peers in their own words. A lecture on the NHS has been delivered for the past three years by a leading Professor of Medicine at Leeds, which reinforces to our students that, although they are at the bottom of the academic pecking order as pre-undergraduates, they are valued enough by academics in their receiving departments for them to give up their time to deliver a lecture designed for them. This is also a good introduction to lectures and provides students with an opportunity to listen, note-take, and, most importantly, engage with the content and ask questions.

Assessments for this project include a **seminar discussion** on aspects of the NHS crisis, for example, staff shortages, shortage of resources, the social care issue, bed-blocking, etc., plus an **annotated bibliography** for a specific essay title on the same issue, which allows students to gain experience in researching different types of texts – newspaper articles, websites, books, academic journal articles – and evaluating them for reliability. It will not be possible to have access to all the above human resources in every institution that provides a foundation programme, but other resources are available to spice up your syllabus. There are plentiful lectures on YouTube or other online channels that will serve the same purpose.

Tutors may worry that the inclusion of subject-specific content might be beyond their capabilities, particularly if students are moving onto degree subjects where the content is not at all familiar or perhaps science-based when a tutor is language/arts trained, for example. It must be made clear that tutors are not expected to be specialists in students' future degree subjects, but rather there to guide and advise the best way to approach the subject from a skills perspective. The best we can do in most EAP scenarios according to Dudley-Evans and St John (1998) is to take an interest in what the students will be studying and try to find out how a discipline works through the analysis of core texts.

Reflective team task

Now you are at the end of this chapter, here are some questions for you and your team to discuss together:

- What kinds of academic culture challenges have you faced with your students? How have you dealt with them?
- Have you noticed any changes in your relationship with your students since the move to online learning?
- Have you begun addressing unconscious bias with your students? How have you managed to integrate it into your syllabus?
- What are your experiences with plagiarism/malpractice? Do you agree with Pecorari (2003) that most of our international students plagiarise unwittingly rather than intentionally?
- What methods do you employ to ensure that students are a) aware of plagiarism and its consequences, b) able to avoid plagiarism, and c) understand how Turnitin works?
- How do you prepare students for life after foundation year?

References

BALEAP. 2008. *Competency Framework for Teachers of English for Academic Purposes*. [Online]. [Accessed 16 January 2019]. Available from: www.baleap.org/wp-content/uploads/2016/04/teap-competency-framework.pdf

Cottrell, S. 2001. *Teaching Study Skills and Supporting Learning*. Basingstoke: Palgrave.

Culture Plus Consulting. 2018. *'A-Ha' Activities for Unconscious Bias Training*. [Online]. [Accessed 1 June 2018]. Available from: 'A-ha' Activities for Unconscious Bias Training | Include-Empower.Com (www.culturepusconsulting.com)

Dudley-Evans, T. and St John, M. J. 1998. *Developments in English for Specific Purposes*. Cambridge: Cambridge University Press.

EHRC (Equality and Human Rights Commission). 2016. *Widespread inequality risks increasing race tensions, warns EHRC*. [Online]. [Accessed 27 August 2021]. Available from: Widespread inequality risks increasing race tensions, warns Commission | Equality and Human Rights Commission (www.equalityhumanrights.com).

Pecorari, D. 2003. Good and original: Plagiarism and patch-writing in academic second-language writing. *Journal of Second Language Writing*. **12** (2003), pp317–345.

TEDx Talks. 2013. Inclusion, Exclusion, Illusion and Collusion. [Online]. [Accessed 20 August 2019]. Available from: Inclusion, Exclusion, Illusion and Collusion: Helen Turnbull at TEDxDelrayBeach.

The Higher Education Academy. 2014. *Addressing Plagiarism*. [Online]. York: The Higher Education Academy. [Accessed 5 May 2019]. Available from: https://s3.eu-west-2.amazonaws.com/assets.creode.advancehe-document-manager/documents/hea/private/resources/addressing_plagiarism_1568037222.pdf

The Nursing and Midwifery Council. 2018. *The Code: Professional Standards of Practice and Behaviour for Nurses, Midwives and Nursing Associates*. [Online]. London: Nursing and Midwifery Council. [Accessed 7 January 2021]. Available from: nmc-code.pdf

2 Syllabus design

Relevant BALEAP competencies:

Student needs:
5. *An EAP teacher will understand the requirements of the target context that the students wish to enter as well as the needs of students in relation to their prior learning experiences and how these might influence their current educational expectations.*

Syllabus and Programme Development:
8. *An EAP teacher will understand the main types of language syllabus and will be able to transform a syllabus into a programme that addresses students' needs in the academic context within which the EAP course is located.*

(BALEAP, 2008)

Initial considerations

There are several different theoretical ways of approaching syllabus design, which Charles and Pecorari (2016) discuss at some length, but which we do not wish to go into in great depth in this practical guide. However, we follow social context-based approaches to EAP in which students become socialised into their discipline community as they are 'exposed to disciplinary practice' through reading, listening to lectures, writing reports, etc. Therefore, slowly they start to think, act, speak, and write in ways that are appropriate to their field (p50). This approach sits particularly well within content-based teaching or ESAP, but may be different from your teaching context. To read more on the wider context of EAP teaching, how it started, what has influenced its development and direction, and starting out as an EAP practitioner, read Ding and Bruce (2017) *The English for Academic Purposes Practitioner: Operating on the Edge of Academia*.

The syllabus is a very important and practical document as it contains all the detail of how the course fits together. In fact, as Charles and Pecorari say 'much of the success of a course depends on what happens before teaching starts…' (2016, p60). So, it is crucial that the syllabus is well planned. Cottrell (2001) points out that the development of skills has become increasingly important to employers and the government and, therefore, to educational institutions. Providers of education have looked at what key skills are needed and for ways of facilitating them. Cottrell (2001) explains the idea behind skills development is that 'deep learning' occurs where students are more likely to retain and use a skill rather than 'surface learning', which mainly involves memorisation, which traditional testing and examinations tend to evoke. The emphasis on skills development is one where the learner begins to utilise a particular skill independently rather than being able to recite any factual content. In this type of learning environment, then, language is not the primary focus of a course but a sub-set of a particular skill. For example, if a learning outcome is that a learner needs to be able to think critically, tasks that facilitate this should be built into the syllabus alongside the language needed to express criticality. This is a more integrated approach to syllabus design. Skills and language are not isolated things; we only ever use language for a purpose, so any attempt at teaching language without a context would not be realistic or particularly helpful.

Charles and Pecorari (2016) list the following as initial considerations for syllabus design:

> *Needs*: What do the students need in terms of skills and language to successfully cope with their future degree studies? What level do these skills and language need to be at by the end of the IFY course?
> *Learning objectives:* What do students need to be able to *do* by the end of the IFY course?

Charles and Pecorari (2016) are very clear that learning objectives should be things students know how to do and when to do them rather than knowing facts; a skills-based approach. They also say that learning objectives should be sequential, with no gaps, so that means that what IFY students can do by the end of their course is what they will need to begin their degree programmes.

> *Constructive alignment:* Harmonising course content, assessments and the learning objectives. (Biggs, 1996, cited in Charles and Pecorari, 2016). For more on this, see Chapter 4 of this guide.

The key areas for syllabus design, according to Charles and Pecorari (2016) are timing and delivery, teaching and learning, assessment and materials. We will look at each of these in detail in this guide. However, before we do that, let's take a look at the BALEAP competency framework (2008) at the start of this chapter. There is a certain degree of overlap in the framework, which is inevitable when attempting to deconstruct something that is naturally inseparable in a sense. When designing a syllabus, for example, all of the elements need to come together in order to provide the most appropriate course of study for the students and to deliver it in the most appropriate way. However, arguably, the two most pertinent BALEAP competencies here are those relating to student needs and to curriculum design stated above.

First steps in programme design

So, with these descriptors in mind, the first step in programme design is to define your target participants. This will be important to determine how you pitch the course. Who are your students going to be? What are their interests? What do they already know?

Are you likely to have a multi-national or single nationality cohort?

Clearly, there *are* going to be some differences between learners, which Cottrell (2001, p23) describes as patterns of 'inhibited and motivational responses'. These are made up of six levels, including 'beliefs' and 'identity'. Part of what the learner comes to the learning with will be as a result of their cultural and religious upbringing, which may impact on the way you do things; both in terms of syllabus design and content, and also in terms of delivery and classroom activities. In terms of syllabus design, it is the designers' responsibility to be aware of some of these important cultural and religious sensitivities.

In addition to these factors, Ryan (2012, cited in de Chazal, 2014) identifies three kinds of shock: *culture* shock, *language* shock, and a*cademic* shock, which can result from a change to the learners' new environment. These are also relevant factors to keep in mind when designing a syllabus as well as when teaching international students.

Obvious examples of cultural influences are those associated with religion. As anyone teaching Muslim students will be aware, the month of Ramadan is where believers are expected to fast for long periods during the day. This can make students more lethargic and perhaps affect their concentration span, especially in a country such as the UK where the daylight hours are very long and therefore make fasting even more taxing. So, where possible, factoring such occurrences as this into your syllabus design would be beneficial, particularly in a mono-cultural context. However, Ramadan, like Easter, is a moveable event, which might mean that it is not always possible to avoid certain assessments, examinations, or deadlines, but at least by being aware it may be possible to create a more flexible syllabus that can change to accommodate such events in the calendar.

Another example of a cultural factor can be the way in which students from particular countries have been taught previously. Cottrell (2001, p21) refers to 'equilibrium' where the learner is satisfied with the manner in which they think. What then happens when the learning environment changes can cause 'disequilibrium' where the learner becomes aware of their limitations in their thinking and as a result becomes personally dissatisfied. Given all the possible emotions learners are likely to experience in competency five of the BALEAP Framework (2008, p6), it is stated that course providers need 'knowledge and understanding of the prior learning, expectations and values that students are likely to bring from their original learning culture'. This better enables course providers and teachers to provide supportive learning environments.

An example of this might be that in China it is traditionally common to have very large class sizes with more of a rote learning focus than communicative language teaching approach. This type of educational system can lead to students who are reluctant to form, let alone to voice, their own opinions in a whole-class exchange. The same students, however, often speak much more freely in small groupwork or pair work, in our experience. Such considerations don't necessarily mean that whole-class discussion work should be avoided entirely, but that they may fall flat and, therefore, not take up the duration it was expected to or planned for. It could mean that you may need to scaffold group discussions carefully or lead up to whole groupwork gradually over a period of time in order to avoid situations where there is complete silence in a classroom, and the aims of the session cannot be met. Therefore, thinking about these potential pitfalls during the syllabus design process could be beneficial to the smooth running of the course.

In our experience, putting the two cultural groups together mentioned above generally means that Middle Eastern or European students tend to dominate in any oral work and are generally much more confident and outgoing but, when it comes to writing, they have much to learn from Far Eastern students. Often students from the Far East have a good grasp of grammatical accuracy and are generally suited to written activities where they have time to think and rephrase.

Clearly, you have to think about the cultural composition of your cohort and decide how you will allocate or split your groups as some conflicts may also occur between particular nationalities. This might be a matter for consideration at the syllabus design stage or simply one of classroom management when relevant and keeping in mind those three types of shock (Ryan, 2012, cited in de Chazal, 2014) mentioned above.

Some issues between different nationalities stem from long-standing hostilities and historic events, and you may feel that certain content or topics should, therefore, be avoided altogether. However, situations can also change over time, depending on what's happening in the world at large. So, it's useful to try to keep up with the news and respond sensitively wherever possible and appropriate both in terms of materials design and adaptation.

Mono-lingual or multi-lingual groups?

The mother tongue or tongues of your cohort is also another factor to consider when designing your course since this is a factor that is most likely to determine the kind and the quantity of language work. For example, you might have some students in the cohort who speak English as a first language alongside those with perhaps only sufficient language to be accepted onto the course. The first group may need very little in terms of grammar or fluency work and simply need input on academic style and register. Whereas the latter group may need to work on accuracy and fluency in addition to academic style and register. Both groups of students are likely to need to be introduced to academic English. You may have second language speakers with a variety of first languages and there will most likely be various levels of English proficiency in the cohort in general. All of these factors will affect the syllabus design in terms of language input and may invoke academic and/or language shock in your students (Ryan, 2012, cited in de Chazal, 2014). These various types of shock are coupled with the effects of disequilibrium where learners are dealing with feelings of loss of face and humiliation in front of their peer group, possible anxiety about failure, and a range of other negative emotions, thoughts, and feelings.

It is reasonable to assume that students affected by shock and/or disequilibrium are less likely to perform to the best of their ability and therefore might take longer to assimilate and integrate into the new learning environment; particularly, as Cottrell (2001) points out, if the learner also becomes resistant. Therefore, any actions that you can take in order to reduce the impacts of shock or disequilibrium would be helpful.

For example, where you have mono-lingual cohorts there may be some benefit to building in occasional translation activities or to using the mother tongue in some circumstances. In the pure form of the communicative method, second language use, or 'code switching' in the EFL classroom, is frowned upon. However, as Charles and Pecorari (2016) point out, new research looks on 'translanguaging' as a more positive thing. However, whether or not you will be in a position to incorporate any such activities into your syllabus will also depend on whether your teachers are all bi-lingual in the students' first language.

How old are your students likely to be and what age range is your cohort?

Age can be another factor that affects how you design your course because, for example, younger learners may have limited experience in critical thinking, unlike someone older who is likely to have had more life experience and, therefore, more experience in problem solving and reflective practice; perhaps with a touch of realism or cynicism thrown in for good measure. However, older learners could have become more entrenched in their behaviour and attitude towards learning. They may be more resistant and, therefore, suffer more from trying to adapt to a new learning environment.

However, whatever the age of your learners, critical thinking plays a pivotal role in academic life in the UK context and should therefore be a key component in an IFY course. In fact, de Chazal (2014, p121) identifies it 'as one of the defining characteristics of EAP'. The question as to whether critical thinking is a separate, teachable skill in and of itself or whether it is an integral part of most other skills has been debated but, for us, it is the latter approach that we take. In fact, it could be argued that it is one of the most important skills as we consider that one of our primary objectives is often teaching students how to think. Therefore, critical thinking is included wherever possible in our worksheets and materials and it is important to allow sufficient time in the syllabus and lesson plans for that to take place under the guidance of the teacher, who can ask leading questions in order to encourage its development.

In addition to these issues, very young people may not know certain things about the past. For example, a group of students taught recently had no idea who won the Second World War but, rather than be surprised, we should ask ourselves 'why should they know this?' Considering their age and if they come from the Far or Middle East, because, even though the Second World War impacted the whole world, it was and still is a Eurocentric and age dependent topic. Giving consideration to decolonising the curricula in terms of materials/content selection is covered elsewhere in this book. However, for now suffice to say that where you have a wide range of age groups represented in one class, it may mean tweaks to topics in your syllabus are necessary.

Technology: Friend or foe?

In our experience, the students coming through our IFY module now are very different from previous years' cohorts. With the advances in technology, it is now common practice for students to bring laptops or phones into class with which to access materials, take notes, etc., and we actively encourage this as part of our paper-less, green strategy. We currently house all our module materials on Minerva, which is a virtual learning environment. However, there are some drawbacks to this as the students seem to be more easily distracted these days. They are often actively messaging friends and family during class, doing their online shopping, or engaging in other non-study activities and occasionally even take phone calls during classes or lectures. It seems that the youth (Millennials and post-Millennials) are programmed to multi-task rather than focus on one thing and therefore tend to find it very difficult to give anything their full and undivided attention. They seem to need to change activities quickly and it is now common for lecturers to include regular breaks in their lectures in order to accommodate this.

We find that our students don't generally tend to read – even for pleasure – and therefore find it genuinely 'shocking' (their word) when they find out how much they are expected to read on their courses. In fact, as far back as 2001, Cottrell states that learners may find reading more challenging than teachers think and yet, in her book, there is only one chapter devoted to reading while there are three on writing. We suggest that more emphasis be placed on reading when students are coming to university without much experience of reading long texts. Your syllabus design may need to incorporate tasks to encourage the development of the various reading skills and strategies needed for academic study. Therefore, you may need to allow more time for introducing students to timed reading activities and other techniques for reading than perhaps you might once have considered necessary. Skimming and scanning and reading for gist are, however, ways of avoiding reading in a way so time also needs to be given to developing intensive reading skills.

Other issues are that technology sometimes lets us down. There are times when the university's server is down, which means that there is no access to Minerva, our virtual learning environment. Clearly this can be problematic if it is the only means of accessing course materials. So, if these things are within your control, try to ensure that the technology can support your decisions about how and where to store, and to deliver, your course materials.

One interesting issue we discovered is that, when we send students back their work with annotations and feedback, if they open these on their phones, they often can't see the annotations. I believe this depends on how they elect to open the document but, if students fail to realise there *are* annotations throughout the main body of their work and only read your final comments, you are doing a lot of work for nothing; as they cannot respond to comments you have made if they have not seen them. So, if you are marking work via computer and using tabs to create annotations, you will need to communicate to students that they need to read *everything* you have written. Ironically perhaps, marking through Turnitin, online, makes it easier for students to see all the annotations and comments, as long as the server is up and running at the required time.

Whatever your own thoughts and beliefs are about the technological age, you will need to recognise that what is described above is probably the reality of your current student body, and Covid-19 certainly speeded a change in the way we all delivered in 2020. Now that these practices have become the 'new norm', there is, in my view, no going back. The bell cannot be un-rung, and indeed some changes have proved to be very successful. Therefore, it is most likely that hybrid modes of delivery will be the future of EAP, in the UK at least, and you will need to decide how you are going to deal with these things going forward. Are you going to embrace technology or reluctantly acknowledge its place? However you decide, you will need to think about the place of technology in relation to your syllabus design and materials delivery. Flipped classrooms, for asynchronous learning, for example, with synchronous sessions more for consolidation activities, is one model which you may adopt. If you are back in a face-to-face situation, are you going to approach activities such as note-making in a traditional way using paper copies or are you going to allow them to do this on their phones or laptops, as they probably will in reality?

Division of groups by language level

Language, as we have previously touched on, is a key consideration for syllabus design. However, as we have previously said and as Davies points out

(1990, p138), language cannot be taught or tested in isolation as it is 'not divorced from communication'. Therefore, it is not the only element of a syllabus, but nevertheless it is an important one for the EAP context.

As such it might be the factor you use to spilt the cohort; having different classes for different ability levels (such as intermediate, upper-intermediate, and proficient). If you choose to split your cohort in this way, one advantage is that the group is fairly cohesive and therefore no one should get left too far behind or leap too far in front of the rest. It makes it easier for the teacher to plan, pitch, and pace a lesson. All the students should be more or less making progress at the same rate, in theory at least. In practice, this has not been the case in our experience as the performance of the whole group in each task in each lesson will not always be consistent. Some of the more committed and more engaged students will normally make more rapid progress overall than those who are not, irrespective of language level, supporting the view that progress and success are attitudinal to a large extent.

As well as thinking about the language levels of your cohort, you will also need to consider what the minimum language requirement for entry onto your course needs to be, as well as what level the bulk of your cohort will be at when they start your course and what exit level is required. Clearly, the lower the minimum entry requirement in language, the more difficult it can be to get those students up to the level of achievement they need to demonstrate by the end of your course. So, you need to be realistic in your expectations of what students can achieve academically given that language may be a handicap to their progress.

Most university students are vetted according to IELTS levels, with different schools and faculties within institutions having their own standard entry requirements, and these can also vary between institutions. In our context, students have often needed to exit our module with the numeric equivalents of straight As or a combination of As and Bs in all their modules in order to progress onto their chosen degree course. These other modules are *content* modules (in combination with our study skills module), which don't measure their level of English, and they are not required to retake an IELTS exam to prove their level of English again at the end of the year.

However, the conditions for accepting students onto degree programmes at our university are not always the same as our internal conditions for every organisation feeding students into our university programmes. Some private providers are required to put their students through IELTS at the end of their foundation year programmes but, because we are part of the university, our internal provision is generally trusted as being appropriately rigorous and quality controlled not to need an additional test of language such as IELTS.

The content module assessments are not measuring language specifically; even our module does not purely do that. We do look at language as a separate part of assessments, as you will see in other parts of this book, but we do so in conjunction with a range of academic skills and content. It should be noted here that the level of (English) language a student has is not a concise indicator of their academic abilities. Much of academic study success centres on critical thinking, time-management skills, and an ability to understand and follow instructions. In saying that, students do need to have a sufficient level of English to cope with the course content, so the two things are connected at least to some extent. However, in the past we have had L1 English speakers or proficient speakers who have not successfully completed our module either because perhaps they did not have the academic capabilities or because they did not see, despite our best efforts, the need for studying on our module. They thought that, because they could speak the language, they should be allowed to go straight onto their chosen degree without understanding the need for them to acquire the skills to support them in their future studies. In other words, IFY assists academic literacy development and in turn shows them how to become members of their academic community.

There were things we incorporated into our module in an attempt to counter the view that IFY is a waste of time, and one in particular that does seem to work. You may wish to consider including a similar task in your syllabus.

Open book exam – week 1

We find that some students feel that they are too good, or too well qualified, to benefit from anything we might do with them on our academic skills module. This aligns with de Chazal's statement that 'where EAP is not needs driven it is likely to be because the students do not yet know why they are learning English and are likely to be younger' (2014, p175). Although we are not simply teaching them English, this theory applies equally, if not more so, to them sometimes not understanding the nature of our study skills module. Often students think they are on a language course, which they don't need or they are simply not aware that they do not have the necessary academic and study skills already. So, a few years ago, we introduced an open book exam in the very first week of the course. This takes place under timed conditions in the classroom without any opportunity to prepare beforehand. They are given an essay question to answer: they first need to listen to something, take notes, read a couple of short texts, and then write an answer to a set question in the form of a 500-word essay. We don't require them to write a reference list, but otherwise we ask that they use information from the sources and cite them in their essay. This is not designed as a test of content and we tell them this (hence no need to revise anything), but it does help us to make an assessment of the current level of their academic skills and language. Having done this timed task, they generally, very quickly, see that there are things they can learn and therefore are inclined to be more receptive to our teaching.

Below is an example of a complete timed essay task, but please note that we have not included the sources. You will need to find one appropriate video source of approximately 15 minutes duration and two texts of approximately 600–800 words; all need to be on the same topic and all containing at least some information that they can use to answer the specific essay question you set beforehand.

Timed essay instructions

You are going to write an essay based on the listening and reading material, which will be provided to you in this paper.

Task 1: Essay planning

You will be given five minutes to consider the following essay title, before you watch a short talk and then read extracts from some articles about the same topic.

> **Essay title:**
> *Explain what is meant by 'environmental health' and discuss how human health can be affected by specific environmental factors. Illustrate your answer with examples.*

What is the essay title asking you to write about? You have **10 minutes** to consider this question, which will help you prepare to write the essay later. Your tutor will tell you when you should begin this task.

Write your notes and plan on the answer paper given.

Task 2: Listening and note-making

Watch a 15-minute talk entitled …… and *make notes on your answer paper* of the key points that you think are relevant to the essay title.

Task 3: Reading and note-making

Extract 1

Source

Extract 2

Source

Task 4: Essay writing

Using the notes you have taken for Tasks 2 and 3, write a short essay of 450–500 words based on the essay title above (Task 1).

> You must base your essay on the listening and reading material (Tasks 2 and 3) and include accurate references to the sources of your information within the text of your essay. However, there is no need to write a list of references at the end of your essay. You should follow the Harvard system of referencing. You must support your ideas with references to information from the listening material (Task 2) and each of the reading materials (Task 3).
>
> Please write your plan for the essay and your essay on the answer paper.

Additional benefits of the timed writing task

The timed writing serves two other purposes for us in addition to motivating students to think about the academic skills and language they need in order to complete this task well. It also gives us a sample of each student's written language, which we keep as a record in case we need it as evidence in any plagiarism or malpractice meetings. Lastly, we also use it as a reflective tool in semester two. Once they have been introduced to and had opportunities to practise various academic skills, such as those mentioned above, in semester two we let them look again at their original essay from week 1 of their foundation year journey and compare it to what they now know. They are often quite surprised, and sometimes outright shocked, at the naivety of their earlier selves.

Below is an example of a worksheet we have used to revisit the timed writing task from semester one.

> **Revision of academic skills**
>
> **Task 1: Thought cloud**
>
> In small groups, try to create a concept map or plan of all things that should be included in an academic essay. Think about structure, language, and content.
>
> Here are some items to start you off:
>
> - Topic sentences – use to introduce the subject of each paragraph.
> - Conclusion – a summary of the main content of your writing.
> - Relevant content – select content that answers the question.
> - Be explicit – explain links between content/point and how it relates to the question.

Task 2: Selecting relevant content

- Look at the mock exam essay question from the start of the year.
- Listen to the recording and read the texts on environmental health.
- Make notes as you listen and read to help you answer the essay question.

Task 3: Self-evaluation of your writing

Using your first essay on environmental health:

- Read your essay and evaluate to what extent you answered the question.
- Write down three positive and three negative things about your essay.
- Now reflect on the progress you have made so far this year.

Task 4: NHS Formative Essay

Now look back at your NHS essay. Take ten minutes to read through it again before you think about the questions below:

- Which part of the essay-writing process took up most of your time?
- What do you think is the best part of your essay? Give reasons.
- What do you think you have improved upon since the essay you wrote back in September? Reflect on the progress you have made this year.
- What do you think you still need to work on for your next written assessment?

Share your thoughts with other students and compare your progress.
Now, exchange your essay with another student. Using the questions below as 'criteria', read the essay and give each other feedback:

- Has the student fulfilled the task, that is, answered the essay question?
- Does all of the content appear relevant?
- Are ideas supported with clear examples?
- Does there appear to be some analysis of the topic rather than just description?
- Are paragraphs structured clearly (perhaps look at one in some detail)?
- Is the overall structure clear – introduction, main body, conclusion?
- Is the essay written in an appropriate academic style?
- Is the use of grammar and vocabulary accurate?

- Does the reference list appear to be written correctly? Is it in alphabetical order? Do the references cross-reference correctly with the citations?

Task 5: Self-study action plan

Tell a partner:

- what you have discovered about yourself and your writing
- what you still feel you need to do some work on
- what you are going to focus on in your self-study time as a result of today.

Grouping by chosen degree area

Apart from grouping cohorts according to their English language level, it is possible to group them according to chosen degree area instead. The ESAP approach is very much the approach we have taken at our university recently. As explained earlier, we now have four IFY modules: Academic Study Skills for Medics and Dentists, Academic Study Skills for Arts and Humanities, Academic Study Skills for Business, and Academic Study Skills for Science and Engineering, with the content for each module being specific to the discipline area. This is easier to achieve where the students are all progressing onto the same or similar degree areas but, in other cases, there may be a wide range of degree destinations. However, what is practical about splitting cohorts in this way is that assessment tasks can be designed around what the specific requirements of those departments are. For example, if a degree includes assessed reflection, it makes sense for us to also include reflection into our teaching even if this is not summatively assessed at foundation level.

It would not make sense though to include a summative examination, for example, in our assessment package if students never do any examinations as part of their degree. Some students, such as Engineering students perhaps, are not required to demonstrate critical thinking in their writing in the same way as students of Arts or Humanities subjects may be required to, and rather than writing essays they may spend their time writing factual lab reports. In other words, critical thinking may look different in different disciplines. If the cohort is split by discipline, assessments can be matched directly to the skills and language students will need in order to successfully study on their chosen degree programme.

The washback effect of targeted discipline-specific assessment should be that each of the skills, sub-skills, and language required in each of those discipline-specific assessment tasks should be taught on the IFY module. Essentially, washback refers to 'the impact which tests have on teaching professionals, test takers and educational environments' (Manning, 2016). The effects can be either positive or negative but, when testing has a beneficial impact on what happens in the classroom, this is seen as positive washback. (If you wish you read more on this, Manning (2016), chapter 11 is all about washback.)

The relevant skills, sub-skills, and language can be *formatively* (i.e. developmentally) assessed so that students are given every opportunity to develop the skills and language they need for use in their future studies. In other words, syllabus design should start from the identification of, and build in the development of, the necessary transferable skills and language for their studies and their future careers.

Of course, whether or not you can do this by splitting the cohort into different modules or whether you do this by splitting the same cohort into different groups within the same cohort depends to a large extent on how many students you have in total on your foundation programme. There are obviously minimum numbers of students to make one viable teaching group and you will have to work within these limitations at your institution.

Content-based vs language split

If your cohort is too small to split into discipline-specific modules or groups, you will probably need to use language level to split them. In this case, you will not be able to focus on the development of skills through content specifically from their subject areas, but will need to use more generic content for this purpose; in other words, an EGAP approach. Before we went into content-based teaching, we used to use generic content, we believe, very successfully. The topics we chose for our projects were taken from a range of contemporary global issues. Since there is no shortage of issues in the world today, this is a relatively easy choice, but one that encourages students' critical thinking skills since they are things that affect them in their day-to-day living. Some of the topics we have covered include: food security, energy security, natural resources, Corporate Social Responsibility, English as a global language, health, urban regeneration, and urban development.

Although we acknowledge that not all students will be interested in all of these topics, the same can also be said for their interest in topics taken from their chosen degree areas.

The danger of doing content-based topics from their own areas is that you can, sometimes, unwittingly, duplicate things that are covered by the academic staff in the department. When that happens, students usually begin to complain about repetition and teaching staff in the department in question may not take kindly to their material being covered, sometimes, as they see it, wrongly. As Charles and Pecorari (2016, p9) tell us, 'the applied nature of EAP means that ... the EAP practitioner is positioned between the students and the subject specialists ... and must negotiate rather complex relationships with them'.

Syllabus design

This takes us back to the argument about content-based teaching and whether or not EAP can be or should be ESAP or EGAP. Hyland (2006) is a proponent of ESAP, whereas Freak (2011) argues for an EGAP approach, but you can read more about these two approaches in de Chazal (2014). The issue of the complex relationship with subject specialists particularly applies to ESAP, in our experience. Following the ESAP approach begs the question of the extent to which the EAP teacher should be an 'expert' in content. How much content knowledge you consider to be sufficient or necessary for teaching skills and language is the biggest question to try to answer before you sit down and plan your ESAP syllabus.

Learning outcomes

You will need to establish what the learning outcomes will be for your course. What do you want students to learn as a result of completing your course? What will they need in order to study autonomously successfully on their chosen degree course?

Below you can find an example of the learning outcomes from an IFY module:

Learning outcomes

If you attend and complete all of the coursework satisfactorily for this module, it is expected that, by the end of this module, you should be able to:

Reading

- read authentic texts in English at a suitable rate
- take clear notes
- select appropriate information for a particular purpose

Listening

- attend to details in a lecture or presentation
- take effective notes
- attend to details in a discussion on a complex reading or listening
- understand proficient speaker speech at regular speed, if not overly idiomatic

Writing

- structure ideas coherently in an essay or assignment
- discuss a topic in an essay or assignment

- develop an argument supported with examples from multiple sources in an assignment
- communicate effectively without serious interference from grammatical mistakes
- refer appropriately to sources in-text and compile a bibliography correctly

Speaking

- actively participate in a seminar discussion
- clearly deliver a presentation of up to 15 minutes
- communicate ideas with minimal interference from grammatical or pronunciation errors
- actively participate in a spontaneous discussion

Language

- differentiate between academic English and other genres
- select appropriate vocabulary for a task
- understand the conventions of an academic style.

1 Skills outcomes

1.1 Leeds for Life skills

This module develops the following Leeds for Life skills:

- **Research skills** – when writing your essay for this module, you will need to identify the most relevant sources of information, read them closely, and understand how they relate to one another. This develops your research skills, which are essential in every field of academic study.
- **Reasoned argument** – in your assessed essay, you will need to put forward a convincing, rational, and well-supported argument. This involves the development of core skills in a wide range of disciplines and tasks.
- **Time-management** – this module requires you to submit assessments to set deadlines. By planning ahead to ensure that you have enough time to complete your work on both this module and other modules to a high standard and meet the deadlines, you will be developing your time-management skills.

36 *Syllabus design*

1.2 Employability skills

This module also develops and demonstrates your employability skills, including:

- **Interpersonal skills** – in classes on this module, you will improve your ability to debate issues effectively, respectfully, and productively. In almost any job, you will need these same skills when attending meetings, both within your organisation and with external clients.
- **Oral communication** – while discussing ideas with others in seminars or delivering a presentation to the class, you will be developing your skills in effective oral communication. These are essential workplace skills, both in formal meetings and in informal interactions and discussions.
- **Managing projects** – by successfully submitting your assessed work on time, you will demonstrate your ability to manage a project independently from conception to completion. Employees who can be trusted to work independently and deliver the expected outcome are highly valued in all career contexts.
- **Reflective writing** – this is a skill required by employers in the health sector as it demonstrates that you are able to reflect on your experiences, identify your strengths and weaknesses, and improve upon your performance. You will be developing your reflective writing skills throughout the academic year.

After taking this module, you will be in a position to put these skills down on job applications, talk about them in interviews, and go on to use them in the workplace. You can see further examples of employability skills that you are developing across all of your modules in School of Languages, Cultures and Societies (LCS), and tips for using them in job interviews, here.

Once you have set your learning outcomes, you will need to check your syllabus to make sure that:

a   You address each one of them at some point during your course.
       Clearly, *all* of your aims should be met by your course content, materials and tasks.
b   That you build in some recycling in order that students can practice and develop specific skills.
       Given the fact that skills are acquired gradually over time, it is unreasonable to expect to introduce something and then the students immediately do it. For example, referencing is a complex skill involving the

mastery of the mechanical system of recording the reference information correctly and citing in-text appropriately. However, the more difficult aspects of referencing such as when and how to use support in their writing, where and how their own voice should come into their work if they are expected to always use support, and how to synthesise from sources are skills that need much longer to develop fully and therefore need a lot more recycling throughout the year.
c   That your materials are appropriate to the student level and meet one or more of your learning aims.
   When looking at content there may be many apparently suitable materials out there and it is easy to lose sight of the skills and language focus if you are not careful. Whether or not a text or video can be used to focus on a specific skill or sub-skill is the question to have in your mind when searching for sources. Be aware that it can often take a long time to find exactly the right audio, video, or text and this time needs to be factored into any workload allocations for materials development.
d   That your assessments also reflect your learning aims and that the assessments reflect what has been taught on your course/your course reflects what will be tested in the assessment tasks. In other words, that you do not assess anything that has not been taught or is not one of your learning aims.
   What is taught in class, the materials used, the assessment tasks created, and the learning aims of your course must all connect together so that what you say you want them to learn is what they need and therefore what you teach. All of these should be what is measured in your assessments so that your course is fully coherent but over-assessment or duplication of assessment of learning outcomes should be avoided.
e   That students always have the opportunity for practice, and formative assessments *always* precede summative ones.
   Anything that you plan to assess should first be taught. Students should always have the opportunity to experience the 'thing' first and reflect on that in order to develop their skills and language.

The progression of the syllabus

Once you have decided what your learning aims and types of assessments are, you will need to look at the time available for teaching and build your syllabus according to the level of complexity and need. For example, you need to teach paragraph writing *before* they have to write a paragraph. They need to know how to analyse essay questions *before* they start planning. So, you would cover both of these things before asking students to write an essay. Using the writer's own voice in writing or creating an argument is more complicated than writing a topic sentence. Therefore, it makes sense to cover topic sentences *before* looking at voice or argumentation. In other words, look at your syllabus and design it logically, and gradually build in more complexity and more learner autonomy as the year progresses. For example, you might start with teacher-led discussions and move on to student-led discussions. Given that one aim is to develop learner autonomy, you might guide students more at the start of the year on, for example, their self-study priorities and then gradually reduce the amount and frequency of scaffolding in the syllabus and leave them to work out what they need to do through self-reflection. For more on this, see Chapter 7.

Dates and deadlines

The number of teaching hours available will also determine how you approach syllabus design and the calendar will predetermine at least some of your deadlines and cut-off points. For example, the date Easter falls upon or other moveable holidays will have to be worked around in terms of deciding hand-in dates for assessments, marking and return of marks. One tip we have to offer in this fairly complicated process is that you put yourself into each person's shoes. So, imagine you are a teacher trying to do what you require. Is it possible to do this by your deadline? If you don't think you could do it, your teachers probably can't either. Similarly, put yourself in the place of your students and ask the same question. Of course, this also to applies to yourself too. Can you meet your self-imposed deadlines? If not, you will need a rethink.

External factors, such as the availability of rooms or external speakers or educational visits, may also affect the way your syllabus is rolled out. There is not much you can do about these things sometimes except to make it all as manageable as possible within the constraints you have. These are likely to change each year and, taking into account any student or teacher feedback, you will need to revise, adapt, and amend as necessary before the start of each new academic year.

Acting on feedback

There are three places where we get feedback on our module; the students, the teachers and the External Examiner. All these perspectives are different and valid, but. in our experience. need to be considered on their merit and whether or not they really would improve our module.

In our university context, students are asked to complete a National Student Survey with pre-set questions. The relevancy of one or two of these is questionable since they previously asked students questions such as 'was the content intellectually engaging', which is clearly directed towards a content-focused programme not a skills and language development course. Although these standards are not always applicable within this feedback, we look to see if there is anything we should act on. This can be difficult at times as, often, one piece of feedback counters another. For example, some students can see the value of peer feedback but others want a teacher to tell them everything.

Where there are strong pedagogic reasons for something, such as peer feedback, we don't typically make any changes to our module. There are usually negative comments about the times and duration of some classes. Over the years, students have told us they don't like classes to start at 9.00 and they don't like three-hour classes. We tell them that there is nothing we can do about issues like that because, well, we can't.

In addition to the mandatory National Student Survey we also organise a focus group of students who meet with us at the end of the year and discuss the various elements of the course, what worked, what didn't. This gives us much more specific feedback to work with.

Teachers' comments are often very useful because they have not usually been directly involved in the syllabus design and are therefore much more detached and objective. However, sometimes teachers have particular pet peeves, so it is important to work out where others stand on the same point to decide whether or not there is any real need for change.

Teachers are more likely to spot things as they teach throughout the year and, in our experience, it is better to change them at the time or make very good notes about what the issue is otherwise it can fall by the wayside at the end of the year/start of the next.

Similarly, the External Examiner's perspective is an interesting insight into what your course looks like from the outside. Sometimes, a simple fix is all that is required. For example, one of our External Examiners felt that having specific rubric for each assessment was confusing for teachers. So, we asked them. They told us they weren't confused but, in fact, found it useful to have specific descriptors that matched the specific task. So, we kept all the various rubric and made the justification for doing so clear to the External Examiner.

Another one wanted the trail to the final mark to be much more transparent, so we added more detailed comments to the moderation forms so that he could see more of our conversation, thought processes, and how we ended up at our final marks.

Now you are at the end of this chapter, here are some questions for you and your team to discuss together:

- To what extent is content important in developing skills and language in an IFY context?
- What are the positive aspects or ESAP/EGAP?
- What are the constraints of ESAP/EGAP?
- How do you feel about the use of the students' first language in mono-lingual groups? Why is this?
- What impact does language proficiency impact skills development?
- What is the most appropriate balance between skills and language teaching?
- Are stereotypes helpful or harmful in EAP teaching? Why is this?

- How important are attitude and self-motivation to successful learning?
- Are there opportunities for autonomy to be fostered in your students? Is this important? Why is this?
- How transparent is the constructive alignment of your programme to students? Is this important? Why is this?

References

BALEAP. 2008. *Competency Framework for Teachers of English for Academic Purposes*. [Online]. [Accessed 16 January 2019]. Available from: www.baleap.org/wp-content/uploads/2016/04/teap-competency-framework.pdf

Charles, M. and Pecorari, D. 2016. *Introducing English for Academic Purposes*. Oxon and New York: Routledge.

Cottrell, S. 2001. *Teaching Study Skills and Supporting Learning*. Basingstoke: Palgrave.

Davies, A. 1990. *Principles of Language Testing*. Massachusetts, USA: Blackwell.

de Chazal, E. 2014. *English for Academic Purposes*. China: Oxford University Press.

Ding, A. and Bruce, I. 2017. *The English for Academic Purposes Practitioner: Operating on the Edge of Academia*. [Online]. [no place]: Palgrave MacMillan. [Accessed 18 March 2021]. Available from: www.vlebooks.com/Vleweb/Product/Index/1018399?page=0

Manning, A. 2016. *Assessing EAP Theory and Practice in Assessment Literacy*. Reading: Garnet.

3 Materials development

Relevant BALEAP competencies:

Student critical thinking:
6. *An EAP teacher will understand the role of critical thinking in academic contexts and will employ tasks, processes and interactions that require students to demonstrate critical thinking skills.*

Student Autonomy:
7. *An EAP teacher will understand the importance of student autonomy in academic contexts and will employ tasks, processes and interactions that require students to work effectively in groups or independently as appropriate.*

Syllabus and Programme Development:
8. *An EAP teacher will understand the main types of language syllabus and will be able to transform a syllabus into a programme that addresses students' needs in the academic context within which the EAP course is located.*

Text processing and text production:
9. *An EAP teacher will understand approaches to text classification and discourse analysis and will be able to organize courses, units and tasks around whole texts or text segments in ways that develop students' processing and production of spoken and written texts.*

(BALEAP, 2008)

In-house material design

Materials naturally follow on from syllabus design and this is where the detail happens. Of course, there are many different coursebooks on the market, but we find that writing our own materials enables us to tailor content and activities to suit our specific context in a way that using a coursebook cannot provide. Similarly, the other option is to supplement coursebook material with your own materials, however, we prefer to use in-house materials exclusively. This ensures that our module is unique as well as best fitting students' needs.

There may appear to be an overload of BALEAP competencies above but the reason they are all here is because the materials writing stage is where all of these competencies need to be considered. A colleague of mine recently likened good practice in EAP teaching to the 'eat-well plate'; where one needs a certain balance of proteins, fats, vitamins, and minerals in order to maintain health and well-being. The EAP 'teach well plate' should be designed as a smorgasbord of language, skills, and competencies delivered in combination and in an integrated, cohesive way. Materials should, of course, meet the learning outcomes for the module and equip the student with the necessary tools to function in their chosen discipline, as discussed elsewhere in this book.

An introduction to study skills

Foundation courses are exactly what the name implies. They should focus on the necessary key skills, language, and competencies students will need to be able to cope with their future studies. However, as Cottrell (2001) suggests, any skills-based course can hope to achieve little more than introducing students to skills because it takes time for learners to be able to apply them to various situations in order to practise and develop them. This is undoubtedly true, not least because, as Cottrell (2001) also points out, students don't always appreciate the usefulness of the skills until they are actually in a position where they need to use them and maybe encounter difficulties. This only really happens after they have left IFY and started their degree programmes.

The basic principles we employ to materials design are topic-based, task-based, and skills-based. We write worksheets with the view that language is a functional resource for the communicative purpose. De Chazal (2014, p17) points this out when he says that 'ultimately, EAP assessments are based around skills and meanings rather than either knowledge or the demonstration of discrete language items' with topics being 'narrowed down in EAP and focused on in more depth, from different **perspectives**' and that 'students need to engage with meanings in texts through skills and activities…' (de Chazal, 2014, p13). If we agree that this is the purpose of assessments, as we do, it is also the purpose of teaching materials. The rationale for this view of language is very much borne out by writers such as de Chazal (2014) quoting Carter and McCarthy in 2006, who point out that there is nothing unique about academic English in terms of the structures of English grammar not found anywhere else. Therefore, it makes sense to integrate language functions into worksheets as and where appropriate rather than building skills work around language acquisition.

Critical thinking skills

We have said elsewhere that critical thinking is a key skill in academic life, but is one that is underdeveloped in our learners. As de Chazal (2014, p12) points out, 'to engage with the academic world, critical thinking skills are vital…'. He goes on to say that 'EAP materials need to be designed around the development of critical thinking' and this is very much our approach to materials design. Our understanding of education means doing something extra with the information provided than simply retelling. So, whatever skills and language worksheets you produce, always try to build in activities that will facilitate analysis, evaluation, and understanding, not simply description, identification of facts, or memorisation.

Below, you can find an example of a worksheet where students are asked to think carefully about what they are going to read *before* reading, then to compare their own conclusions with those in a text on the topic. This means that they will be looking for specific information in the text, but doing more with it than simply repeating it or listing facts. You will also see that the worksheet provides language that students may require in order to be able to perform certain functions associated with developing a discussion.

Worksheet 1 Top myths about wind energy

Task 1

Your tutor will give you a number of statements about using wind to generate energy. In groups, discuss them and decide if you think they are true or not. What are your reasons for believing/not believing the statement?

Statements:

A   Building a wind farm takes more energy than it ever makes.
B   Installing wind farms will never shut down power stations.
C   Wind farms harm property prices.
D   Wind farms are dangerous to humans.
E   Wind energy needs back-up to work.
F   Tens of thousands of wind turbines will be cluttering the British countryside.
G   Wind farms should all be put out to sea.
H   Wind farms are noisy.
I   Wind farms won't help climate change.
J   Wind farms are inefficient and only work 30% of the time.
K   Wind farms negatively affect tourism.
L   Wind power is expensive.
M   Wind farms are ugly and unpopular.

N   Wind farms kill birds.
O   The UK should invest in other renewable energy technologies and energy efficiency instead of wind power.

Task 2

You will now be given information to read about some of the myths associated with wind energy. What is a myth?

Task 3

Match the information to the statements you have been given already. Which statements were *you* correct about?

Task 4

Now you are going to practise **orally refuting** statements with your partner. One of you will make a claim about wind energy and the other will refute it. Use the 'myths and facts' from the article you have read. Try and paraphrase the language from the article.

For example: (using 1)

Student 1:

'*It could be argued that* if wind energy is used, the countryside will be ruined by thousands of turbines.'

Student 2:

'*However*, according to the British Wind Energy Association, only 3,500 additional wind turbines are needed to deliver 8% of the UK's electricity. Moreover, approximately 1,500 of these would be placed offshore.'

Useful language

Introducing your claim...

It	could be	said	that...
		maintained	
	might be	claimed	
		stated	
	may be	argued	
		asserted	

Refuting...

However,
Actually,
As a matter of fact,   according to X...
May I point out that...

                According to X...   ... it seems clear that...
                                   ... evidence seems to
                                               suggest that...
X   seems to suggest that...
                    points out that...

Now practice with your partner.

Source: The British Wind Energy Association (n.d.) Wind Energy: Top myths about wind energy. In Donellan, C. (2005) *Energy Matters*. Cambridge: Independence Publications 97:15–17.

Below, you can read the notes written for teachers giving the rationale and proposed lesson plan.

Worksheet 2 Top myths about wind energy *suggested procedure*

Task 1:

The purpose of this task is to give students the opportunity to discuss what they think is true/believable about wind energy. Give them time to discuss each statement and to try and think of supporting reasons.

Task 2:

Elicit what a 'myth' is.

Task 3:

Allow students to read the article from the British Wind Energy Association and ask them to match a statement with the relevant paragraph. Ask them which statements they thought were true.

Task 4:

This particular task looks at refuting claims. There is some useful language given and, in pairs, students could take some of the points from

46   *Materials development*

> the article and practise making claims and refuting them. Encourage paraphrasing and summarising.
>   Alternatively/Additionally, they could each prepare an oral summary of one of the points to present to the rest of the class.
>
> *Students could also pay attention to the **style of referencing** in the text, using footnotes. You could ask them to practise ways of incorporating the reference within the text.

Recycling skills, competencies, and language

Over the year of the Study Skills Foundation module, we aim to recycle as much as possible so that students have as many opportunities as possible to practise applying the same skills and competencies to different tasks. Just how much recycling you can do will depend on the level of difficulty a particular group or cohort are having with the skill or competency in question and the duration of the course overall. On the IFY programme at Leeds, for example, we have an academic year with the same cohort but on pre-sessional courses this time can be as short as six weeks.

The form the recycling might take can also vary. It may be useful to build in practice of a particular skill in both oral and written tasks and this is essential for critical thinking, as we have previously discussed. For example, you may pose discussion questions to explore their opinion or prior knowledge of a topic or issue. However, given their age and experience, we find that often IFY students don't have the life experience to put forward differing views or to think of potential arguments for and against, for example. Therefore, it can be useful to allocate various roles to students (either for or against a particular topic) and ask them to read or watch something in order to find arguments and evidence for their position on the issue.

The following three worksheets demonstrate how students can be given scaffolding into the arguments for and against wind farms before taking part in a discussion. This particular topic was one we used several years ago when it was a current issue.

In Worksheet 3, the students listen to a recording of the BBC's *Coast* programme made through the university's licensing agreement. This provides an introduction to the topic and some of the basic arguments for and against wind farms.

In Worksheet 4, they listen to *Countryfile*. Again, a BBC programme recorded under licence. This recording provides more detailed arguments into wind farms and extends the students' knowledge in preparation for Worksheet 3.

Worksheet 5 is where students discuss the situation in a structured way, enabling them to practise forming and developing logical arguments and refutations, and making judgements about the validity and merit of arguments and counter-arguments.

The students are allocated roles from the five possibilities in the worksheet, which look at the issue from slightly different perspectives. Prior to the discussion starting, they spend the first 20 minutes gathering and selecting their evidence and deciding which arguments to present to the meeting. These arguments are taken from the materials from the earlier worksheets and the RSPB website, so they are practising using evidence from sources. As you can see, the way the worksheets are structured also requires them to utilise their reading and listening skills, as well as note-making and working in groups, integrating skills into an, arguably, 'authentic' task.

This approach falls in line with BALEAP (2008, p8) competency 10 'Teaching practices'; stating that EAP teachers should be able to 'integrate study skills into other skills teaching', competency 6 (BALEAP, 2008, p6) 'Student critical thinking', where it states that EAP teachers should 'provide opportunities and stimulus for critical thinking in sequences of learning activities'. Also, that EAP teachers 'will employ tasks, processes and interactions that require students to work effectively in groups or independently as appropriate'. Thereby, developing study skills together with the development of student autonomy and critical thinking.

Before the discussion can take place, the teacher needs to allocate roles, according to the number of students in the class, in order to form small groups for the discussion. It might be that not all five roles are required but each discussion group should have a balance of perspectives on the issue so that there is scope for some genuine discussion to take place.

The teacher will also need to decide whether smaller groups will discuss simultaneously or individually, and, if the latter, whether the rest of the class will be present or not. There are advantages and disadvantages for both. Where small groups are discussing simultaneously, the teacher will need to move between the groups and, therefore, won't be able to catch everything, whereas, if groups come individually, the teacher can observe each discussion unfolding in its entirety and better monitor individual performances. However, when groups are not in class, this time needs to be filled productively.

Teachers might also want to give all those with the same role some time together before the start of the discussions to compare their approach/arguments etc. This can be especially useful for students the first time such tasks are being undertaken.

Worksheet 3 Isle of Lewis case study

You are going to watch an eight-minute report about a wind farm that was proposed for the Isle of Lewis in 2006. Lewis is the largest island in a group known as the Outer Hebrides, which are situated off the north-west coast of Scotland.

As you watch the programme, make notes on the following:

1. factors that make Lewis 'an attractive location for commercial wind farm developers'
2. the reason why the turbines need to be so tall
3. statistics relating to the claimed benefits from the wind farm
4. statistics relating to the size of the wind farm
5. the reason why, according to the developers, the farm needs to be so large
6. arguments against the wind farm.

Worksheet 4 Isle of Lewis case study

You will watch a second report on the proposed wind energy project on the Isle of Lewis, in which you will hear more detailed accounts of the arguments for and against the project.

Task 1

As you watch the report, make notes on the various arguments which are put forward.

Task 2

Working with a partner, compare your notes and rearrange these into the most logical order. Where possible, match opposing arguments on each aspect of the project and its potential effects.

Worksheet 5 Isle of Lewis case study

Although the 181-turbine wind farm project was rejected, there is now a proposal for a wind farm of 53 turbines on the Isle of Lewis (RSPB, 2010).

Role A: Scottish Executive

1. You and your partners are members of the Scottish Executive, with responsibility for chairing a public meeting in which detailed arguments for and against the proposed wind farm project on the Isle of Lewis will be heard.
2. At present the area is protected under European law, but you have the power to authorise the construction of the wind farm if you judge that there is an overriding public interest in this.

3   At the end of the meeting, you will be given five minutes in private to consider your decision, which you must then give to the meeting.
4   You have 20 minutes before the meeting begins to discuss what information you will need in order to make this decision.

Role B: Isle of Lewis Tourist Board

1   You and your partners represent the Isle of Lewis Tourism Association, whose members are all involved in the local tourism industry.
2   You have been asked by the Scottish Executive to attend a public meeting at which the arguments for and against the proposed wind farm project will be heard. At the end of the meeting, the Executive will give its final decision on whether to allow construction of the wind farm.
3   The Isle of Lewis is famous for its scenery and wildlife, which are the main reasons why people visit the island. You believe that the proposed wind farm would have a devastating effect on this and the lives of local people who depend on tourism for their living.
4   You have 20 minutes before the meeting begins to discuss what information and arguments you wish to present.

Role C: Lewis Wind Power Ltd

1   You and your partners are directors of Lewis Wind Power Ltd, the company that is planning to build the wind farms on the Isle of Lewis.
2   You have been asked by the Scottish Executive to attend a public meeting at which the arguments for and against the proposed wind farm project will be heard. At the end of the meeting the Executive will give its final decision on whether to allow construction of the wind farm.
3   You have strong personal belief in the value of the wind farm project. You also have a duty to your company's shareholders to do everything you can to ensure the project is allowed to proceed.
4   You have twenty minutes before the meeting begins to discuss what information and arguments you wish to present.

Role D: Royal Society for the Protection of Birds (RSPB)

1   You and your partners are campaigners from the RSPB.
2   You have been asked by the Scottish Executive to attend a public meeting at which the arguments for and against the proposed wind farm project on the Isle of Lewis will be heard. At the end of the meeting, the Executive will give its final decision on whether to allow construction of the wind farm.

> 3 You have 20 minutes before the meeting begins to discuss what information and arguments you wish to present.
>
> **Role E: Scottish Highland and Islands Regeneration Agency**
>
> 1 You and your partners are member of this Agency, whose purpose is to find ways of ensuring the sustainable development of local communities and the economies on which they depend.
> 2 You have been asked by the Scottish Executive to attend a public meeting at which the arguments for and against the proposed wind farm project on the Isle of Lewis will be heard. At the end of the meeting, the Executive will give its final decision on whether to allow construction of the wind farm.
> 3 You have 20 minutes before the meeting begins to discuss what information and arguments you wish to present.

Facilitating group bonding through materials

When your students first arrive, it is unlikely that many of them will already know one another. As Cottrell (2001) says, in order to create a safe learning environment where students feel able to speak out, try new skills and language, and not feel too anxious or afraid about being wrong or losing face, it is important to build activities into your early classes to get to know one another. We have done this by using *Padlet*, which is a noticeboard that students can all add to. Obviously, there are other similar online tools and other ways of doing this. If you have the same classroom for each lesson, for example, you might be able to use a physical board, which students can add to. We add our details first, show students the board with our entry already on it, share the link with them, and ask them to add a photograph, together with their name, nationality, language(s) spoken, and one or two of their likes and dislikes. Sometimes students are reluctant to share photographs, perhaps for religious/cultural reasons, but if they do add one, it is so much easier to put a name to a face for the teacher as well as the other students.

Another activity you could use is to put students in pairs to get to know one another. You then ask one of the pair to introduce the class to their partner. This can be a good way of beginning the process of learning one another's names and listening to what others say.

Creating belonging opportunities through materials

To introduce yet another BALEAP competency here, number 5 'Student needs' refers to 'the use of tasks and materials that incorporate a variety of learner roles and learning styles' (BALEAP, 2008, p6).

Changing the pairings and groupings can assist with group relationships and dynamics. The actual logistics of this will be the responsibility of the teacher in terms of their classroom management, but you will need to incorporate opportunities for creating group bonding and belonging into your classroom materials. The more students work with different people, the more likely it is that they will feel comfortable in the group as a whole. If a student always sits with the same person, it is likely that they will repeatedly share the same perspectives and opinions with the other. Working with different people can give food for thought and different ways of looking at the world maybe previously not considered by the other partner. However, it doesn't always work to move people as sometimes personalities clash, but doing so at the start of the course is a positive thing as this is also a learning time for the teacher in terms of group management. Knowing who not to put together is equally important as knowing who compliments others or works in similar ways. However, include opportunities for movement into the classroom materials so that teachers are encouraged to think about how to move students around.

Maintaining motivation through materials

Moving students around can also help reduce boredom and loss of concentration. This also applies to changes in tasks and activities. So, do try to build some variety into your worksheets. Including a variety of activities and tasks also allows for accommodating different learning styles within the group. However, in general, students will probably also need to develop their concentration spans so sometimes it is acceptable to spend most or all of a class doing the same sort of activity, such as listening to a lecture, developing a discussion or seminar, or reading a text. There will still be a mix of sub-skills within each specific skill. You may start the year changing activities more frequently, when students are perhaps feeling overwhelmed, than towards the end of the first semester or the year, for example. Another potential motivator is the content of projects and tasks. Try to identify topics that will interest your learners. For example, our nurses, dentists, and medics will encounter the NHS in their practice. Therefore, we have included a project about the NHS to give them some necessary background prior to starting. Other EGAP IFY provision may find global issues as motivating as our previous cohorts did. Educating students on natural resources, energy supply, and food security has the added benefit of drawing attention to these problems in the hope that the generations to come can tackle some of them in a positive way.

Initial materials: Managing expectations

BALEAP (2008, p4) competency 1 'Academic Contexts' states that:

> *'An EAP teacher will have a reasonable knowledge of the organizational, educational and communicative policies, practices, values and conventions of universities'.*

52 *Materials development*

With this in mind, consider building in a session to talk about mutual expectations at the start of the year. We agree with Cottrell (2001) that it is important to do this. As we have discussed elsewhere, students often come with preconceived expectations that may not be realistic and, if not met, cause unrest and dissatisfaction. Here is how we begin to establish rules and (re)form expectations.

We discuss the following things on the list of teacher expectations with our groups:

* maturity
* enthusiasm for learning
* active engagement with learning
* responsibility for own learning
* willingness to learn from peers
* ability to think critically about information, i.e. ask questions and challenge
* respect for peers, staff, the rest of the academic community and environment.

And what they will be expected to take responsibility for:

* know when and where your classes take place beforehand
* come to class on time and bring everything you need for your lessons
* have completed out-of-class tasks and self-study as required
* actively engage in activities and participate in all the classroom tasks and discussions – even if you are not interested in the topic or task.

Who they have responsibility to:

* your peers
* your tutor
* the wider community

And remember that

* respectful and supportive relationships must be reciprocal
* the university has a strong policy on 'dignity and mutual respect' (see section 3.4 of the university document on this).

What they can do to show maturity and take responsibility:

* listen
* write important information down, e.g. what tasks you need to complete out of class

* manage your time effectively, for example, diary, timetable, prioritise tasks
* visit library regularly – subject area for books and latest edition of journals
* read, read, read – reading lists from department
* ask tutors for help.

The importance of their attitude towards their studies:

* topics you will study
* not all topics will interest everyone
* being engaged and interacting with the topics
* improving your language and academic skills through the topics
* how your assignments will be marked
* comparing your performance with other students.

Learning in class is done together with classmates, not only through the teacher.
    Be prepared to:

* listen to what your classmates have to say
* share information and learn from one another
* remember that there may be cultural differences between you and others
* respect your classmates
* speak in English in class.

Pair or small group discussion helps learners orientate themselves to their new learning context. We ask them to discuss if the following are acceptable or unacceptable behaviour:

1 A student arrives late for classes and lectures.
2 A student switches their mobile phone to silent during classes and lectures.
3 A student chats during classes and lectures.
4 A student shares their opinions with other students during classes and lectures.
5 A student actively listens when other students are talking.
6 A student actively listens when the teacher or lecturer is talking.
7 A student laughs when another student says something wrong.
8 A tired student sleeps at the back of the class or lecture.
9 A student swings on or slouches in the chair.
10 A student throws an eraser etc., across the classroom to another student.
11 A student tells another student they disagree with them.
12 A student tells the teacher or lecturer they disagree with them.
13 A student asks questions during the class or lecture.
14 A student asks questions after the class or lecture.

54 *Materials development*

The following worksheet is an example of how students can be introduced to the values in their discipline. BALEAP (2008, p4) competency 2: 'Disciplinary differences' states that EAP teachers should 'provide students with frameworks to investigate disciplinary differences and values, particularly in relation to the communication of knowledge'.

Worksheet 6 Professionalism in Healthcare

Task 1

What kind of behaviour was expected of you at school? Will this be any different to what is expected at university?

During your training there will be many references to *'professionalism'* and *'professional behaviours'*. What do you understand these terms to mean? Discuss in groups. Write down your definition.

Task 2

Your tutor will assign each of you a document to read about professionalism written by the governing bodies responsible for regulating behaviour in the nursing, dental, and medical professions. Skim read this (do not read in great detail) and note down what is expected from those working in the healthcare sector in terms of being professional.

A Nursing and Midwifery Council

www.nmc.org.uk/globalassets/sitedocuments/other-publications/enabling-professionalism.pdf

- Find a definition of professionalism.
- How do you achieve professionalism?

B General Dental Council Standards

https://standards.gdc-uk.org/

- What does the General Dental Council consider professionalism to be and how is the information organised?
- Look more closely at principle 9. What aspects of professionalism are outlined? What keywords/characteristics are mentioned when you look at the individual standards?

C General Medical Council

www.gmc-uk.org/ethical-guidance/ethical-guidance-for-doctors/good-medical-practice

Access the main page, go to 'view contents', then look at the contents list on the right-hand side of the page.

- What are the four domains of professionalism?
- Look at domain 4. In your own words, what does this cover? Look for keywords/phrases regarding the characteristics expected in a medical professional.

What do you think might happen to a dentist, doctor, nurse, or other healthcare professional if they did not behave in a professional manner?

Task 3

Now discuss how you think these concepts of professionalism might translate to your time on International Foundation Year?

Task 4

As a prospective healthcare professional, you will need certain skills that are additional to your qualifications. 'Soft skills' play an important role. Discuss what we mean by 'soft skills'? Check it in the dictionary if you are not sure.

Task 5

Below are some of the soft skills needed in healthcare:

- empathy
- communication skills
- be a team player
- dealing with pressure
- strong work ethic
- positive mental attitude
- flexibility
- time management
- self-confidence
- dealing with criticism.
    1   With a partner, discuss why these are necessary for someone who works in healthcare. In what kinds of situations might you use these skills? Think about what a dentist/doctor/nurse does.
    2   Do you think these skills can be taught?
    3   How might these same soft skills apply to your foundation year? Discuss in what circumstances you can work on these skills this year?

56 *Materials development*

Below you can find an example of a worksheet that allows students to work with a report for structure. This type of activity orientates learners to the task type and the second task on this worksheet enables them to link what they see to the report they are going to produce for their written assessment.

Worksheet 7 Report structure

Source: Maass Wolfenson, K. D. 2013. *Coping with the food and agriculture challenge: Smallholder's agenda* [online] [Accessed 24 June 2014] Available from: www.fao.org/fileadmin/templates/nr/sustainability_pathways/docs/Coping_with_food_and_agriculture_challenge__Smallholder_s_agenda_Final.pdf

Task 1: Purpose of a report

What are the differences between an essay and a report? Discuss in pairs.

Task 2: Structure of a report

Look at the structure of the 'Smallholders' document and think about the following:

- What sections are included in it?
- How can the reader find information?
- How easy is it to identify the various sections? Why is that?
- What type of referencing is used?

Task 3: Planning the structure of your report

Now think about the report you have to write:

- What is the purpose of your report?
- What sections should you include in your report? Do you need all the same sections as the 'Smallholders' document?
- How should you organise the information clearly?
- What is the most logical order of the information?
- *What type of referencing should you use in your report?*

One way of getting students to begin thinking about categorising evidence or ideas is to offer them the overarching groupings. This way they only have to begin by placing the various bits of information in the correct category. Once students are used to doing this, the next step in the process is for them to determine the categories for themselves. As you can see, the worksheet starts by asking them if they know any of the categories already. They can then check these against the ones given.

Materials development 57

You can also see the section of the student worksheets written in italics refer to referencing. These little reminders should appear regularly to reinforce the importance of referencing and how doing these things fit into working with academic integrity.

Worksheet 8 Five main issues needed to address global food security

Task 1

In the short video you watched, **five issues** that we need to address to ensure global food security were mentioned. Can you remember what they were, and what they mean when we relate them to food security? Discuss this first with your partner.

Once you have done that, go back to the three texts you read over the holidays and try to find examples that are related to each of those issues in some way. Fill in the chart below with the examples you find. *Don't forget to write your citation, as this information may be useful for your report.*

Availability	
Accessibility	
Acceptability	
Adequacy	
Stability of sources	

Source: War on Want position paper. 2011. **'Food Sovereignty: Taking back control of our food system'**.

Task 1: Speed reading and summarising

Using the food sovereignty text:

- Read the introduction and find the cause(s) of the food crisis.
- What is/are **not** the reason(s) for the food crisis.
- Write a sentence explaining the situation in *your own words.*
- Read paragraph 2 quickly and write a sentence *in your own words* summarising what it is about.
- Read paragraph 3 and write a sentence *in your own words* describing the connection between the food chain and countries of the 'global South' and one sentence *(also in your own words)* explaining the

---

58 Materials development

- link between multi-national food companies and food aid and imports.
- From paragraph 4, find the reason(s) for hunger and write a sentence *in your own words* summarising the information.
- Read paragraph 5 for an explanation of the 'Green Revolution'.
- Write a sentence *(in your own words)* explaining what it is and what the connection is between that and small-scale farming.
- Read paragraph 6 and find out why the word *'improved'* is in speech marks.
- Write a sentence *(in your own words)* explaining this and another sentence describing the relationship between agribusiness multi-nationals and farmers' heritage.
- Read paragraph 7 to find out how China is linked to the Green Revolution.
- Write a sentence *(in your own words)* explaining what the purpose of the Green Revolution was and how China's contribution fits into the overall picture.

You can find the rationale given in the teacher's notes for this task below:

*Although there is more to reading than skimming and scanning, some students read very slowly and one exercise in the development of a reading skills and competencies 'package' is to focus on techniques for reading faster. For this reason, make sure that you time students on this task and make sure that they don't try to understand **every** word. It might be easier to do this if you time them reading (1–2 minutes maybe) each paragraph and then time them writing their one or two sentence summaries (1–2 minutes again). Writing a sentence summarising each paragraph should help them to think critically about their reading, begin to identify and select key points, and think about the links between their reading and staying relevant when writing.*

Task 2: Reading, summarising, and making links

Read the section of the text your tutor allocates you and:

- Read each paragraph. As you read, write one or two sentences (*in your own words*) to summarise what it is about.
- Exchange your information with a partner

Discuss the following together:

- how the content of these two sections links together and how this links with the previous paragraphs you read

- how you think everything you have read so far fits into the title of the text
- how you think concentrated landownership might be problematic
- what a price spike is and how that is different from a permanent price rise
- how successful you think the current model of treating food as a commodity to be traded on international markets has been so far
- what you think should be done to meet the needs of *all* people in terms of food security for the future.

Here is the teachers' rationale:

The first part of this task is designed to get them to focus on identifying the theme in a paragraph and the last part of the task is a discussion that aims at developing their critical thinking skills.

Task 3: Reading for specific information

Read the next three sections: 'Food price spikes to permanent crisis', 'Food security: a failed model', and 'Food sovereignty: the positive model'.

Try to find anything that supports what you said in your discussion (in Task 2) or anything that is different from what you said.

Teachers' rationale:

This task is intended to guide them into finding evidence for their own ideas from Task 2.

N.B. Stop them reading at the top of page 6 (at the beginning of the seven principles of food sovereignty) as what follows is a detailed explanation of the principles.

Task 4: Critical thinking

Work in small groups and discuss the following:

- Do you think the food sovereignty system will successfully address the issue of global food security? Give reasons for your answer.

Rationale:

The points they are discussing don't really have any specific answers. The idea is mainly to get them to construct sound arguments and to think.

Note that, although we haven't given the answers to these reading tasks above, on the teacher's copy of the worksheet we do. This is to ensure that all groups are receiving the same answers instead of leaving it for individual teachers to try to work out what they think the answer should be. This helps to facilitate standardisation of delivery of materials.

In the worksheet below, the students are given a link to a report on food security.

You will note that, once again, students are asked to reference the source accurately. As we have previously said, the reason this type of recycling is important is because it takes time to become familiar with the system of referencing (whichever one that happens to be) and students need to be regularly given opportunities to practise doing this *accurately* as often as possible and using as many different source types as is practical. Obviously, if you have less contact time for your course, these tasks can be done as self-study exercises, but peer feedback should be built into any such activities in order to encourage, not only completion of the activities, but accuracy and diligence with every detail of the specific referencing system such as the use of full stops, commas, capitals, brackets, italics, bold, etc. being done correctly. Having another pair of eyes helps identify errors much more easily than if working alone.

In the next worksheet, you will see there are pre-reading orientation questions where students are encouraged to think about what they are going to read in terms of the type of source, referencing, organisation, and the content. Predicting content is a good way of activating knowledge and engaging with the text. This step should be included not just in reading situations, but also before listening text exposure.

In Task 2, students are required to select key information, provide a short summary of this, and to analyse a graph. Students tend to describe or retell rather than summarise or analyse, so, clearly, work needs to have been done beforehand on how to go about selecting key information and also how to analyse a graph. This means interpreting content and data, deriving meaning, and drawing conclusions. These processes require both specific functional language and critical thinking skills.

Task 3 requires students to decide which things are causes as opposed to effects. This is made more complicated in English as either can be presented first in a sentence. For example: 'A lack of access to food results in shortages of fresh vegetables'; 'The scarcity of fresh vegetables is a contributing factor to food insecurity'. Consider also: 'A shortage of fresh vegetables results in malnutrition'; Malnutrition is caused by a lack of access to fresh vegetables'. As you can see in these example sentences, it is not simple and straightforward to decide what role access plays, what role fresh vegetables play, and what relationship they have with one another, to malnutrition, or to food insecurity. Therefore, exercises and activities in identifying cause and effect language are also valuable for IFY students.

In Task 4, students are required to think of solutions based on the causes identified previously. This means that not only should they come up with suggestions, but these should be logical and practical. Again, these critical thinking skills cannot be assumed, especially at the young age most IFY students begin their studies at, so scaffolding and repeated practice will most likely be required.

Worksheet 9 Reading: Selecting relevant information from a report

Task 1: Pre-reading

a   Write a full reference for this source.
b   What are the organisations FAO, IFAD, and WFP, and what is their role?
c   How does the structure of this report differ from the assessed report you will write?
d   How would you find the main points of this report without reading it all?
e   What do you think the three main sections are about?
f   What are you now interested to read more about? Check in *Key Messages* (inside front cover).

Task 2: The current situation

a   Look at p8. Read the text, analyse the graph, and then summarise the current situation.
b   Look at *Key Findings* p12 and note any other significant data.

Task 3: Causes

a   Make additions to the list of all the causes of food insecurity you discussed in Week 1.
b   Which section would you read to find out more about the causes of food insecurity?
c   What are the four 'dimensions of food security' and the suite of 'food security indicators' (p13)? Make additions to your notes.
d   What are the key findings for each 'dimension'? Read pp13–15.
e   What are the key findings for different areas of the world and the factors affecting food security?
f   Note any other significant data in *Key Findings* p17.

Task 4: Predicting and checking predictions

Look at p19: 'The world can end hunger by 2025'.

a   Looking at the causes above, how do you think this can be done?
b   Find the paragraph with examples of action and note them down. Did you predict any of these?

Decolonising the curriculum

Decolonising the curriculum has been very much at the forefront of education over the past couple of years and sector-wide educational institutions are working hard with staff and students to transform what is taught and how it is taught. At the heart of this move is the desire to ensure that education is devoid of racism and is inclusive of the whole student body in the process has been accelerated somewhat since the summer of 2020 and the momentum of the Black Lives Matter movement. To highlight the depth of feeling around this issue from the student perspective, in 2016 universities in South Africa came to a standstill to demand that curricula were decolonised (Meda, 2020).

In our context at the University of Leeds, there have been many university-wide conversations around how we can achieve a more inclusive curriculum, and the university staff and students are currently putting together a decolonisation framework that outlines what we consider our key principles to be. In terms of trying to define what decolonisation of the curriculum means, this is an ongoing debate in itself and the Leeds framework encompasses all types of discrimination in its principles: race, disability, and gender. Advance HE has this clear definition on its website of what a *colonial* curriculum means and what we need to be moving away from:

> *A colonial curriculum is characterised by its unrepresentative, inaccessible, and privileged nature. Unrepresentative, because it selectively constructs teachings which exclude certain, oftentimes, crucial narratives. Inaccessible, because it consequently prevents many of its recipients from identifying with the narratives construed, whilst appealing to a historically favoured demographic. Privileged, because it ensures the continued participation, comfort and flourish of this select group of people, in both an academic and a wider societal context. Sadly, and unacceptably, this all occurs at the detriment of a diverse range of marginalised voices.*
>
> (Advance HE, 2020)

How far you need to decolonise your curriculum may very much depend on your context. In the UK, for example, we are very aware of our colonial past and there has been an awareness that when teaching history in schools and HE it should not be taught purely from the white perspective of power and that students and tutors should be able to challenge this. This may mean revisiting reading lists so that they are not solely occupied by the privileged white male academic viewpoint, for example, so that other more diverse voices can be heard.

So, your first question may be – what does decolonisation mean when we teach EAP and academic skills? What kinds of changes could we implement? Content could be the first consideration. In our case at Leeds, our study skills modules are taught through various projects, and we try to avoid choosing ones that are UK- or Euro-centric in their focus. For example, a previous project on food security involved looking at this issue from a global perspective rather than a local one. The project we now cover with our medics and dentists on the NHS Crisis is, by its very nature, focusing on the UK's health system, but we build in opportunities for students to research and discuss their own, and other global, healthcare systems and make comparisons. We also look at areas such as the diversity of staffing and how the NHS has survived only because of the skilled input of thousands of immigrant workers, from cleaning staff through to surgeons, an area which is often overlooked. When looking at healthcare research, we question global health inequities, particularly those linked to race and gender.

Reading lists are another area for change, as mentioned earlier. Check your module reading list, and if it tends to be dominated by white, male, western academics, then perhaps it's time to include other voices so that you are not missing out on valid perspectives. An issue strongly connected to this is that of 'inclusive citation', whereby staff and students are encouraged to find other voices when engaging in research. Maha Bali, in her 2020 blog on inclusive citation, suggests that academics should ask themselves the following question when researching: '*Are there people working in this field who are women or people of color or non-Anglo?*' (Bali, 2020). Bali also stresses that a diverse module reading list is a way of encouraging students to feel that they can succeed in their field. Seeing someone on the reading list from a similar background as their own shows students that success is possible and that they, too, could become a scholar one day in their field of study. Students should also be encouraged to include diverse voices in their own research. For more information on inclusive citation, see Bali's (2020) thought-provoking blog *Inclusive Citation: How Diverse Are Your References?*

The impact of Covid-19

One of the things that became apparent during the recent global pandemic was that online teaching and face-to-face teaching are very different and that the amount of material one can cover in an online situation is much less than in a face-to-face teaching context. The other noticeable difference has been in the organisation of how those materials have been covered, with many of our colleagues choosing flipped learning as the option for introducing students to subject matter. That is to say, expecting students to engage with materials independently and in an asynchronous manner before their live session and then using the synchronous sessions mainly to check understanding and reinforce learning. Whether or not this was the best approach is not yet clear as more research needs to be conducted into this. However, the way you are delivering your sessions, whether this is entirely online, entirely face-to-face, or some sort of hybrid of the two, will impact the amount of material you can cover. Consideration should be given to both of these factors, ideally at the planning stage where possible. One final point of note is that often students

64 *Materials development*

did not engage with the independent tasks as expected and were joining live sessions unprepared. This negatively impacts the aims of the session and, if session aims are regularly not met, this could lead to the syllabus or learning outcomes not being fully covered by the end of the course. This is possibly an argument for moving away from flipped learning, especially for IFY students, who, because of their age and experience, may not be as capable of the autonomy required for flipped learning to be successful.

Now you are at the end of this chapter, here are some questions for you and your team to discuss together:

- How much of the teaching of course materials is/should be about classroom and personality management?
- How can you know if students' expectations of what and why they are learning are aligned with your own? Is this important? Why is this?
- How important is it for a group to bond with each other? With the class teacher? Personal tutor? Why is this?
- Have you had any particularly positive or negative experiences of group dynamics? Why was this?
- How invested can/should a class tutor be if they have not written the materials?
- How much involvement do you/would you as the class tutor want in writing/adapting class materials? Why is this?
- What 'value added' can/should the class tutor bring to the delivery of course materials?
- How important is it for classroom materials to be accompanied by tutor notes? Why is this?
- How important is it for tutors and students to know the aims of each session? Why is this?
- To what extent do you feel classroom materials can/should be teaching to 'the test'?
- What would you/do you say to a student who just wants to 'pass' the module? Why is this?
- Have you thought about how you might decolonise your curriculum and generally make it more inclusive for all students? Has your institution, or have you as a module leader or tutor, made any changes to what you teach or how you teach it as a result of this? Have students ever challenged you about module content or reading lists? How did you deal with this?

References

Advance HE. 2020. Decolonisation of the Curriculum: A Conversation. Decolonisation of the Curriculum – A Conversation. Advance HE (www.advance-he.ac.uk)

BALEAP. 2008. *Competency Framework for Teachers of English for Academic Purposes*. [Online]. [Accessed 16 January 2019]. Available from: www.baleap.org/wp-content/uploads/2016/04/teap-competency-framework.pdf

Bali, M. 2020. Inclusive Citation: How Diverse Are Your References? 8 May. *Reflecting Allowed*. [Online]. [Accessed 26 July 2021]. Available from: Inclusive Citation: How Diverse Are Your References? Reflecting Allowed (mahabali.me)

Cottrell, S. 2001. *Teaching Study Skills and Supporting Learning*. Basingstoke: Palgrave.

de Chazal, E. 2014. *English for Academic Purposes*. China: Oxford University Press.

Meda, L. 2020. Decolonising the Curriculum: Students' Perspectives. *African Education Review*. **17** (2), pp88–103.

RSPB. 2010. Offshore windfarms and birds: Round 3 zones, Extensions to Round 1 & Round 2 sites & Scottish Territorial Waters [Online]. Bedfordshire: RSPB. [Accessed 26 November 2021]. Available from: https://ww2.rspb.org.uk/images/langston_2010_tcm9-203501.pdf

4 Assessment unpacked

Relevant BALEAP competency:

Assessment Practices:
11. An EAP teacher will be able to assess academic language and skills tasks using formative and summative assessment.

(BALEAP, 2008)

Constructive alignment

As discussed elsewhere in this book, learning outcomes (LOs) are the springboard to syllabus planning and influence the design of both assessments and class materials. 'Constructive Alignment' (CA) is a term first coined by Biggs (1996) and is the principle we apply to the design and development of our IFY modules. Simply put, it is a way of ensuring that students are being assessed on the skills, competencies, and language they need for their future degree programmes, as expressed in the LOs, and that these skills, competencies, and language have all been taught in class or through independent study prior to any assessment.

Above you can see Figure 4.1 shows the interconnectedness of learning objectives, course input, and assessments, which is explored more fully in Biggs (1996); Biggs and Tang (2007 and 2010).

Essentially, the CA model should provide clear, logical, links between LOs, assessment tasks, and teaching and learning materials and activities for both tutors and students. Closing the loop in this way minimises the risk of assessing students on something that they are unable to achieve or are unfamiliar with. The process is something that can and should be discussed with IFY students so that they feel they are in 'safe hands' and are confident that they will not be faced with anything new when the time comes to be assessed. This type of dialogue with students helps to remove the fear of the unknown and, therefore, helps to reduce or alleviate assessment anxiety as it makes the whole process much more transparent. It is also an opportunity

Figure 4.1 Visual representation of constructive alignment.

to explain and remind students that they are not learning in order to pass a test, but so that they are able to transfer and use appropriate, specific skills, competencies, and language as required in the context of their academic study and beyond.

Mapping assessments to learning outcomes (LOs)

The LOs in our context are initially selected after a discussion, or several rounds of discussions, sometimes with receiving departments within the university, regarding the skills, competencies, and language students require on entry to their undergraduate programme of study. These conversations usually centre on the following:

- Issues lecturers/academics in receiving departments may have noticed when teaching international students who have come to an undergraduate programme straight from their previous learning context. This could be anything from poor language control to difficulties adjusting to a new educational culture.
- What skills they would like to see/are most important in first-year undergraduate students.
- The types of assessments they give to first-year undergraduate students.

Time spent discussing these points and building up a good working relationship with teaching staff in receiving departments is invaluable. We have often capitalised on such relationships by inviting them to give content lectures to our IFY students to give them the experience of listening to an expert in their future field of study and to practise their listening and note-taking skills. If your IFY programme is not part of an HE institution, then researching university prospectuses for the LOs and assessment types of relevant degree programmes is a viable alternative and the more conversations you can have with subject specialists the more cohesive the student experience is likely to be.

Developing assessments

Once LOs have been decided upon, and these may already have been agreed by others in your institution, the next step is the design of the assessments and marking rubric. Whoever is writing these needs to decide how all the identified LOs can be met through the assessment 'package'. Again, this is something you may not have control over or be responsible for. Which assessments your students are going to complete may be determined by a particular provider (such as NCUK) if you are a delivery partner. Once LOs have been established, assessments should be checked to see whether they will effectively meet those LOs. Assessments also need to be checked to ensure that all LOs are being met, but also so that there is no repetition of assessment of LOs. LOs need only be met once, otherwise students are being over-assessed. Once that has been done, syllabus design and the development of teaching/input materials can begin.

The academic skills, competencies, and language we focus on are things such as *evaluating* sources, *analysing* essay titles, and *planning* a report/essay. As an example, one of our LOs is to '*think critically* about academic texts and be able to *evaluate* their usefulness and relevance for written and oral work'. This is one of the LOs aligned with our 'annotated bibliography' assessment task, but this is looked at in more detail in Chapter 7.

Lesson aims, scaffolding, and recycling

Again, working back from the bigger picture of LOs, assessment, and syllabus design, the individual lesson or session aims should be scaffolded to aid the learning process. (To read more on scaffolding, take a look at The Bell Foundation website, 2021.)

Taking the LO from above, an example of specific lesson aims might be:

- '*to understand the basic principles of evaluating sources*'
- '*to practise writing an evaluation of a familiar academic text*'.

Evaluation requires criteria against which to judge. In the case of evaluating a source, those most commonly used are reliability, trustworthiness, currency, relevancy. One criterion that our IFY students seem to struggle with is the idea of *relevance* and another is how *current* information is. Generally, *reliability* and *trustworthiness* seem to be easier concepts to grasp, but they still need guided exploration. So, we can say that, in order to meet the lesson aims above, quite a lot of scaffolding of these four criteria in italics is likely to be required before students can successfully evaluate a source. Therefore, input should be recycled in order to allow students to interact with different academic texts and to continue to gradually build and develop their understanding of what *evaluation* means after they have understood the basic principles.

Using the constructive alignment approach, and building in scaffolding and recycling, means that students have multiple opportunities to practise

Assessment unpacked

applying specific skills to various scenarios before any assessment takes place. This allows them to make mistakes and learn from them, and to ask questions leading to 'deeper learning', which is one of the goals Biggs and Tang (2007) aim for learners to achieve through this approach. Deep learning is surely the desired goal of education, where long-term memory is activated and can therefore be utilised indefinitely.

Formative vs summative assessment

You may already be aware of the importance of formative assessment in allowing students an opportunity to practise skills, competencies, and language, and your course may have these built into its design. Your IFY students, however, may not take the same view on their importance and our experience has shown us that, if it doesn't count towards their final grade, students may elect not to do them. There may be good reasons for this, such as workload or overload through bunching of deadlines, but completing formative tasks is an essential step in their learning process and you will probably need to explain this to them.

You have probably heard the distinction made between formative and summative assessment as assessment *for* learning and assessment *of* learning respectively. Both are important but serve different and distinct purposes and you should discuss what these are with your students. It is assessment *for* learning that is the focus for formative assessments and that provides opportunities to develop and hone skills, competencies, and language, and they need to value and to take up these opportunities. (To read more on assessment for learning, see Cambridge Assessment International Education, no date.) However, as we have said above, what is important for you as the tutor to remember is that these things must have already been introduced, appropriately scaffolded, and practised in advance of any formative assessment, and recycling should be built into syllabus design, input materials, and delivery of sessions.

Similarly, formative assessment should always *precede* summative assessment. It is vital to view learning as incremental in this way so that learners are introduced to a 'suite' of skills, competencies, and language through a project, topic, or task, so that learners are given the opportunity to *apply* them to a practice assessment before finally measuring how much learning has occurred. Therefore, summative assessment should come at the end of the project, semester, year, module, but that does not mean it cannot also be formative and developmental. Feed-forward comments on summative assessments can provide a focus for future independent learning.

Preparing students for assessment: What they need to know

There is never any harm in explaining to students the way in which a module operates, and students are usually keen to know as much as they can. As suggested by Moon (2002), information on intended learning outcomes and assessment tasks should always be clearly outlined in the Module Handbook, employing terminology that ensures transparency for students. Transparency in assessment is of particular significance considering students on IFY programmes are under immense pressure to attain the grades they need for undergraduate study and, if they are fully aware of what is expected from them, then you are already beginning to take the first crucial steps as a tutor/module leader towards pre-empting any dissatisfaction with the assessment process.

Ideally, several weeks before a summative assessment, students should be shown the task they will be assessed on, the relevant marking rubric, and where they can be accessed. This advance notice can assist with inclusivity issues such as the clustering of summative assessment deadlines, which often happens in university study. The length of time students receive the assessment in advance may vary, depending on how your content is split and how long your projects/terms/semesters are. Again, this may be determined by the course provider rather than by you, if you are the delivery partner, for example, but the assessment should be released with sufficient time for all students to complete the work necessary before the deadline.

What they need to do

IFY students mostly come to their study directly from school learning contexts and are therefore used to being told what they should be doing and when rather than acting independently. As we say elsewhere in this guide, we see our role as acting as a bridge between school and university expectations, which means that, in order to get them to complete that work, you may need to scaffold their time management by giving constant reminders and mini-deadlines throughout the period. You cannot assume that, because you have given them the assessment, they will start working on it. Often, in our experience, a deadline that is a few weeks away simply means that they put it to the back of their minds and forget all about it, thinking that they will get to it nearer the time, without realising how long each of the steps and stages in completing an assignment can take. Sometimes, they just have to learn the hard way by leaving it too late to do their best work.

Raising awareness activities

Any classroom activities that aid students' understanding of the marking rubric and how assessments are graded are invaluable. Using past examples of student assessment (preferably not on the same topic as you are currently assessing, but the same *type of assessment* or *assessment of the same skills and competencies*) is useful in aiding student understanding of what particular descriptors mean and provides an opportunity to 'translate' them into language they can understand. Rubric tend to be written with tutors in mind rather than students and there is often far too much 'meta-language' making it difficult for students to understand what exactly is required of them in an assessment. Being 'transparent' does not only mean allowing students access to your marking rubric, but also allowing them the opportunity to understand what they really mean.

A real test of a student's understanding of the rubric is when you allow them to 'grade' a student sample. This is something best carried out in small groups with the students having three samples – low, middle, and high – to work with. Give them time to read and understand the task (we have usually taken a similar task to the one they will be attempting, together with the assessment rubric and then, as a group, try to agree on a mark, allowing a few marks either way or at least which band it best fits. The results of this activity can often reveal quite a lot about a student's previous experiences of marking processes or what they perceive a 'good' piece of work to mean. For example, very often students will just grant a mark and when asked to justify it may say that there are language errors. This could indicate that in the past they have been judged on language more than the other skills involved in writing, whereas, on a foundation year skills course, they may need to be reminded that weighting may fall more on other skills, such as organisation of content, using sources to support points, and so on. It also gives tutors an opportunity to tell students that, when we mark, we are always able to justify the mark against the rubric otherwise we are not marking fairly. This activity can go a long way towards students understanding how seriously we, as tutors, take the whole assessment process.

Finally, explaining in some detail the step-by-step process leading up to a submission of work can also help mitigate any nasty surprises for students. For example, many IFY students will never have experienced submitting a draft before or attending a writing consultation where the draft is discussed and may not know what these processes are, or what they involve. One way of dealing with this is to ask students in class to discuss a series of True/False questions to gauge their understanding of these processes and then any misunderstandings can be dealt with reasonably easily. Here is an example of some of the questions you may wish to ask:

- For most of the **written assessment tasks** on the XXX module, you will be asked to produce a plan and/or draft and attend a ten-minute writing consultation with your tutor. For the **oral assessments** (seminar discussion and presentation), you will take part in a 'practice' task beforehand so that you can receive feedback, which will be beneficial for the actual assessment.
- It is important for you to understand what a writing consultation is, and what to expect from it, so that you can maximise the benefits.

Discuss

In a consultation, your tutor will discuss your *essay plan/outline* or *essay draft*, which you have already sent to them. What do you understand by the terms 'essay plan/outline' and 'essay draft'? How are they different?

In order to fully understand how writing consultations work on our module, discuss the following:

Discuss the following statements and decide if they are **true** (T) or **false** (F) or **not sure** (NS):	
It is not necessary to email your plan or draft to your tutor before the consultation.	
It doesn't matter if you're late for your consultation as your tutor has so much free time that appointments can be easily rescheduled.	
If you cannot attend your consultation because you are ill, it is polite to inform your tutor before the consultation.	
Your tutor will fix all of your grammar errors for you.	
Your tutor will comment on every grammar, structural, and content error you make.	
It would be helpful to print off a copy of your plan/draft that your tutor returned to you with comments so that you can write additional notes on it at the consultation.	
It is a good idea to write down any questions you may have about your tutor's comments before the consultation so that you don't forget anything.	
The tutor will lead the consultation and you will sit and listen.	
You may disagree with your tutor's comments/advice, but it is rude to contradict someone with more experience.	
Once you have improved your plan/draft based on your tutor's advice, you will get an A.	
You can email and drop in to see your tutor whenever you like to discuss your work further prior to submission.	

Note, there is no obligation to print off work. Some students prefer to read from a screen and financial or practical constraints might not allow students to print anyway so you should not insist on it. Hence the wording 'it would be helpful …'

Similarly, it should be made clear that it is not a requirement to disclose an illness or the nature of it. However, it is polite to notify the tutor of non-attendance so that they are not sitting around waiting for a student who is not coming.

The true/false questions provide a good opportunity to begin exploring students' current beliefs and perspectives. It is also important to discuss the importance of factoring in planning and drafting time as excellent work is built from sound foundations. Students coming straight from school may not have been used to writing a plan and see it as a waste of time. So, this is a step they can be tempted to miss and may need reminding that having a plan gives them something solid to work from, allows them to self-check and stay on task, as well as to think about and change things that turn out not to work well. A plan should be viewed as something flexible and organic, which they can adapt and change as their attempt at the assignment evolves.

They may also be unfamiliar with the consultation process so, again, this is a good opportunity to remind students that *they* are responsible for leading the session. The tutor has already said everything they wanted to say in their feedback and/or annotations on the work. Therefore, the consultation is an opportunity for students to clarify anything that wasn't clear in those comments, ask follow-up questions, and to leave the consultation knowing what they need to do next in order to refine their work before the final daft is handed in.

They also need to be reminded that, simply by addressing the things they are told to address, it does not necessarily follow that they will get an A or A*. It is the *quality* of the work they produce that determines the final mark.

Managing student expectations

The shift from school to university naturally means that there is a shift in the level of difficulty of study, but this does not always seem to be obvious to students. Elsewhere in this guide, we have talked about the way in which previous learning experiences have shaped individual learners and what they bring with them to the new learning environment. They are perhaps used to scoring very high marks at school, they then move to a university system where they perhaps don't, and this can be quite an 'Academic shock' (de Chazal, 2014) for them. While some students are motivated by a drop in their usual performance to do better next time, others can be demotivated, which may fit in with what Cottrell (2001) refers to as 'disequilibrium' and sometimes in extreme cases may even cause learners to become depressed or anxious. In very extreme cases it may lead to the student dropping out.

Students' perceptions of marks and markers may also be viewed through a particular cultural lens. In their various educational contexts, perhaps they could achieve high marks for simply copying and pasting, as students have told us in the past was the case for them at school.

So, although de Chazal (2014, p191) claims that 'citations are a form of homage to other researchers', the manifestation of this tribute can take different cultural forms.

Indeed, some students have reported to us that they could score as highly as 100% for simply copying and pasting from sources. While this may or may not be entirely factually accurate, it is worth bearing in mind.

'Blame culture'

The issue of 'blame' is by no means unique to international students, as conversations with colleagues in other schools and faculties have shown. When students receive a mark or grade that they don't feel represents what they should have been awarded or that they need, they can sometimes look outside their own performance to find reasons for this. Often, in our experience, with less mature students, 'blame' lands in the lap of the teacher who has marked the assessment. Students compare marks with their friends and their peers and decide that their work was the same quality as someone who got a higher mark. This, in turn, is then perceived as one marker marking harsher than another. The fallacy of the hard marker or the unfair marker is then kept alive by this information being passed on through word of mouth to other students and becomes a difficult misconception to shift. Colleagues in degree-awarding parts of the university told us that students actually sometimes choose their elective modules *purely* on the basis of which teacher is known as a 'lenient' marker.

Clearly this is an unacceptable state of affairs that we need to work to dispel. Two things are important in this quest, first 'face validity' and second 'assessment literacy' (Manning, 2016). First, students; as one of the main stakeholders, need to be convinced about the value of the course. They need to know *why* they are being 'forced to' complete a foundation course when they want to go straight into studying their chosen degree. They also need to understand *why* they are being assessed in a particular way; what the relationship is between what they are learning now in their EAP classes, what they are being assessed on, and why, and how all of this is connected to their future studies. In our experience, students who truly understand these connections apply themselves more wholeheartedly to their studies. It is, therefore, the EAP tutor's role to 'provide pathways into the target learning culture which lead to understanding of its values, processes and tasks' (BALEAP, 2008, p6). In other words, as EAP tutors, we need to have an ongoing dialogue about the importance of becoming a member of their academic discourse community and that is about *how and why* things are done just as much as it is about the content of the discipline.

Myth busting with students

Through transparency

One way of tackling both face validity and assessment literacy with students from the outset might be to spell out to them how markers approach the marking, what the standardisation processes and procedures are for markers, and to explain the role of the External Examiner in ensuring that appropriate quality assurance processes and procedures are in place on your programme.

All students should have access to the marking rubric used for each specific assessment because students should know explicitly what they will be assessed on. This is stated as 'Assessment Principle 13' in Hübner's (2000) chapter on the training implications for language teachers, which arose as a result of funding for accredited courses. Principle 13 goes hand in hand with 'Assessment Principle 12', which says that clear instructions should also be provided, and both of these principles are preceded by Principle 11, which is that assessments should be valid. In other words, they should assess what they say they are going to assess. These 13 principles were established at the time, for what were newly accredited linguistic assessments in HE. However, what is particularly interesting to note here is that, based on observation of assessment rounds, Hübner (2000) echoes other voices, including our own, in noting a lack of training in assessment for language teachers.

One would like to think that those days are long gone now and that lecturers no longer mark according to their own mysterious systems, which are kept strictly secret from students. In general, having knowledge of assessments helps learners to see that the system is fully transparent and fair. Knowledge of what they are being assessed on should assist learners in being more fully prepared for assessment and its purpose. It allows them an opportunity to evaluate and begin to appreciate what they are already proficient at so that they can keep doing those things. This is something learners are often unaware of as they are too focused on what is missing rather than looking at what is present and is, therefore, an area where tutor feedback can be really helpful and is certainly as important as identifying areas for development. Of course, learners do also need to be able to identify their own individual areas for development and, therefore, what they should prioritise to work on in their self-study time. These ideas are included in the definition of what it means for students to be *assessment literate* provided by Manning (2016, p156), where he states that 'an appreciation of assessment's relationship to learning' and 'a conceptual understanding of assessment' are needed. However, as Cottrell (2001) points out, the workings of academia in the UK are often something of a mystery to learners. It is our job as teachers to demystify all of this, or at least as much as possible, for the students and Cottrell (2001) outlines several ways in which this might be done.

First, it is important to explain clearly what is required and why. One hopes that reminders in the form of recycling of the same information at various points in the year can only help these messages be received.

The following example shows how students can be introduced to the different categories of a specific assessment and in this way focus the learner away from one aspect; moving away from exclusively thinking about language, let's say, to a broader way of thinking about assessments. You may or may not want to include any indication of bands if the assessment is formative as it may detract attention from the development purpose of the feedback, as in the second option below.

76 *Assessment unpacked*

ORAL PRESENTATION FEEDBACK *MODULE:*
Presenter: *Date:*
Topic: *Timing:*

Content and organisation	
Support to ideas	
Language	
Delivery	

ORAL PRESENTATION FEEDBACK *MODULE:*
Presenter: *Date:*
Topic: *Timing:*

	100–80	79–70	69–60	59–50	49–40	39–30	29–0
Content and organisation							
Support to ideas							
Language							
Delivery							

Through the use of samples

Another aspect of the demystification process is to develop learners' assessment literacy. Part of the definition of assessment literacy is that students need 'an understanding of the nature, meaning and level of assessment rubric and standards; skills in self and peer-assessment' (Manning, 2016, p156).

Cottrell (2001) suggests that learners should see samples. One tactic to familiarise students with tasks and with marking rubric is to get them to evaluate samples of pervious students' work. Using the rubric in this way helps them to understand the various categories that they will be assessed on and gets them to look in detail at all of the individual descriptors in each criterion in the rubric. Using samples of past students' work also shows them the level expected and that work does not have to be 'perfect' to achieve high marks, as the samples you show will contain some mistakes of one kind or another, be it language, content, referencing, or structural errors. That is one way in which samples are a better tool than model answers. Students can see that the exemplars contain errors and yet may still be awarded high marks. Depending on the samples available, it might also be an opportunity for them to see and discuss different ways in which an assessment task can be approached and may help to foster inclusivity by illustrating different learner styles.

If you are using samples of tasks that are still current, it will also enable students to think about the task they have been set in a little more detail than they might otherwise, and also to think about what they would do the same or differently when they come to complete the task themselves. However, you always need to make sure that you have the necessary permission from the students whose work you are using. Also, make sure not to allow students to take photographs of the samples or to take them away with them at the end of the class, as this might give them an unfair advantage in completing the assessment. This may be a more difficult challenge if you are teaching remotely.

When we use samples with our students, we are often surprised by just how similar their evaluations are to those of the teachers who marked the samples. Perhaps this indicates that receptive skills develop prior to productive skills. It is easier to look at someone else's work than it is to produce one's own. Sometimes, though, we find that they can be harder on the students' work than we are, but, in general, students find this type of exercise is invaluable in developing an understanding of their assessment tasks, the level of work required, and the marking rubric, and is a comprehensive way of familiarising them with the tasks of the 'target learning culture' (BALEAP, 2008, p6). It is a way of taking the abstract into the concrete, working with samples and applying their knowledge of the task and the rubric helps students solidify their understanding of the assessment process. We find that students particularly benefit from seeing a poorly completed task and a task that received high to very high marks. Being able to compare and contrast two (or more) samples of significantly varying quality shows them the range of levels and the kinds of things not to do as well as what they might conclude to be relatively easily achievable.

Through the use of prediction

In line with the BALEAP TEAP competency framework (2008), we aim to encourage our students to become autonomous learners and one of the tools we use to this end is teacher feedback. So, obviously, we want them to look at their feedback carefully in order to work out what they did well and what they need to do better so that they understand exactly *why* they got the mark they were awarded. The idea is that they can use this knowledge either to maintain or, more likely, try to improve their mark for the future. However, students can, frustratingly for us, ignore our feedback and concentrate solely on the mark or grade. This is somewhat at odds with Hübner's (2000) tenth principle, which suggests that students value feedback. Unfortunately, this is not always true, but where feedback is not well received it could be due, in part at least, to their age and level of maturity or to previous leaning contexts. Often, we have found that students mistake critical evaluation with criticism. As Stone and Heen point in their publication 'Thanks for the feedback', it is 'interesting when we give feedback, we notice that the receiver isn't good at receiving it. When we receive feedback, we notice that the giver isn't good at giving it' (p3, cited in Winston, 2017).

And yet, as we know, feedback is vital to development. As Race and Brown, (1995, cited in Hübner, 2000, p96) point out, 'feedback to learners is probably the most crucial ingredient in any recipe for successful learning'. So, another tool we sometimes use to get the student's focus off the mark and onto the reasons behind why they achieved the mark they did is to withhold the mark for one of their formative assessment tasks. We send the annotated work back to them with our feedback comments; usually in the form of three things they did well and three points for improvement. The student must then look very carefully at the annotations and comments in conjunction with the specific task and marking rubric in order to predict the mark that they think the teacher's comments indicate. They have to send us an email telling us what mark they think they have been awarded before we give them their actual mark. This little exercise sharpens the minds of both the teacher and the learner because they must both be aware of the language used in the different bands. For example, *excellent* use of ... belongs in the A/A* bands whereas *satisfactory completion* of ... indicates a D band mark; which is a low pass on our IFY module. (See also Chapter 7, where this is discussed in relation to the annotated bibliography.)

Assessed seminar discussions

Seminars are often used as part of a programme of study nowadays, but receiving schools at our university often comment that international students do not participate in such sessions. Group assessment is now also a common means of assessing students as this type of task replicates many working environments where the workforce work in teams and, therefore, target employability skills. In other words, assessment types that focus on employment and the use of transferable skills and competencies may be assessment types that IFY learners have not encountered in their previous educational contexts.

Building and development of skills, competencies, and language is especially important when thinking about unfamiliar assessment types such as assessed group seminars and therefore need careful scaffolding. Of course, discussing the reasons why they need to be prepared to talk in seminars, as mentioned above, is also important so that they understand why and when these skills might be utilised.

As we have said, the effect of any assessment type should facilitate the requirements of a particular task 'washing back' into the teaching and learning, which takes place before the assessment. (To read more on washback, see McKinley and Thompson, 2018.) Therefore, if we take assessed seminars as our example here, the skills, competencies, and language needed to perform in a seminar need to be unpacked, scaffolded, and systematically taught and recycled, but they can be conducted in many different ways. They can be done in large groups, with or without a lecturer or other member of staff present. Participants may be required to deliver a short presentation to the other members of the group or to lead the seminar, which may require preparing specific questions in advance. However academic seminars are conducted, though, they will usually be based on some pre-reading text or texts. These could be oral or written texts but, whatever the case, students will need to come to the seminar having read what they should have read and be prepared to do whatever the seminar requires.

Academic reading circles (ARCs)

In order to begin to develop some of the skills, competencies, and language required for successful group seminar participation, we start with academic reading circles (ARCs). These were developed by Seburn (2015) for undergraduate students (Pinard, 2015) in order to try to facilitate deeper learning and involve investigating a text from a number of different yet interrelated perspectives.

Below, you can find our worksheets that introduce students to ARCs for the very first time. We have included the notes for teachers here also and the theme of the text for discussion is on the topic of plagiarism, which helps reinforce academic integrity at the same time as developing reading, speaking and listening skills, competencies, and language. These worksheets have been adapted and amended using Seburn's (2015) original concept as the starting point and his work is appropriately acknowledged in our materials. You will see that, because this is the first ARC of the year, the duties of each role are also explained, but this type of scaffolding can gradually be reduced each time an ARC is timetabled.

Organising ARCs

ARCs can be conducted in a face-to-face or in an online context, but more than one opportunity should be provided for students to take part in ARCs as their understanding of them will develop over time. If possible, it is useful to allow each student an opportunity in each role as the ultimate goal of the roles is to show learners that they need to look at each text from *all* of these different perspectives simultaneously each time they approach a text.

In our experience of conducting ARCs, the most successful way is to schedule small groups (ideally groups of five so that you have one student in each role) to an individual time slot, with the tutor present. The tutor should inform the group that they will try to purely be an observer, but that, if things go too far off track, they will need to intervene. One of the things that typically does happen in the first ARC especially is that the students talk about the topic rather than discussing specific points that are in or arise from the text. If that happens, you will need to steer them back to the text. They might be good at talking anecdotally, but the aim is to gain a deeper understanding of the content of the specific text. As the tutor, you should come to the ARC prepared with your own questions on the text in case you need to take over the leader role. The tutor's job at the end of each ARC is to give feedback on the group performance but, before you do that, you should start by asking for students' own perceptions of how well it went. You might find it useful to have prepared questions for this in advance too.

One of the things to watch out for during an ARC is whether or not students are really having a discussion. What can happen is that students are too focused on their role to actually discuss spontaneously. They should be reminded that the point of an ARC is to have a *discussion* based on the text and that the roles are there as a guide for the kind of purpose and perspectives to consider in their discussion. It does often take students a while to get the balance right, though, which is why they need multiple ARCs built into the syllabus.

Various methods of conducting ARCs

As you progress through various ARCs, you can conduct them in different ways and you may choose to end with students running them completely independently of tutor involvement. This will depend on the extent to which you feel them to be capable of such autonomy, of course. Remember IFY is about *beginning* the journey to autonomy, not the end of it. Obviously, if you are working on a project, ARCs are a good way to incorporate a variety of different texts on the topic of a specific project and possibly a variety of source types, depending on the subject in question. As students receive more input on a specific topic, the easier they find the role of connector.

It is also possible to have multiple groups doing their ARCs at the same time. However, this can prove challenging for tutor monitoring purposes. It is impossible, for example, to judge the development of a whole ARC when you are dipping in and out of different groups or you may miss a particular student's contribution and think they haven't participated. So, do think about what kind of feedback the learners need at different points in the development process.

Reading

Introduction to academic reading circles (ARCs): Tutor notes

Aims:

- To introduce students to the concept of academic reading circles.
- To explain the basics of the five roles required for an ARC and what they involve.
- To understand that a text offers more information if read for specific purposes.

This is the introduction to ARCs, the purpose of which is for students to receive a general understanding of the kind of information they can and should be extracting from an academic text. They should also receive a basic understanding of what the different roles involve in an ARC. The goal of this reading task is to get students to recognise that a text offers a great deal of information if read for specific purposes. These perspectives reflect the ARC roles they will be assigned in future. As students learn more and more skills, extra 'duties' may be added to each role.

Task 1

Working with a partner, discuss the following questions:

What kind of reading have you done in the past? Think about how much you read, what you read, and which language you read in.
Are you aware how much reading you will have to do at university?
How do you think this reading will differ from what you are used to?
 Will all be in English/volume will be heavier/will be academic in style.
When you read the text you were given in the previous session, how does it compare to reading you have done before?
What did you learn from this text? *This may be just content information, students may not, at this stage, look further than that.*

Academic reading is very different to reading for pleasure and you will need to use skills such as skimming and scanning for relevant information, evaluating evidence, identifying author arguments and then making clear, well-organised notes if you are planning to use your reading for an academic essay, report, or presentation.

Task 2

Work in pairs or small groups with the text you were given to read and answer the group of questions your tutor directs you to. Move on to the next group of questions when instructed to do so.

Group 1: *Leader*

Write a full reference and in-text citation for the text.

(Duty: finding out the reference information.)

Hart, M. and Friesner, T. 2004. Plagiarism and Poor Academic Practice – A Threat to the Extension of e-Learning in Higher Education. *Electronic Journal on e-Learning.* **2** (1), pp89–96.

What do you think is the most important point to remember from this text?

(Duty: summarising the main idea.)

Which students are most likely to 'cheat'?

(Duty: conceptual question.)

> *Male rather than female/non-mature/less able students/students with an 'instrumental attitude towards education/those with high self-esteem/science rather than health or education students/those who care more about a high grade than actually mastering the subject matter'.*

Why has there been a rise in plagiarism?

(Duty: conceptual question.)

> *Students no longer have a sense of academic integrity/have not learnt the correct rules for citation and referencing/poor time management/ lifestyle pressures/more use of internet 'where acknowledgment of sources is not a priority'.*

What are the policies for dealing with plagiarism?

(*Duty: conceptual question.*)

Warnings and penalties put in place by institutions/investment in detection software such as Turnitin/changing nature of assessments each year and have assessments that demand evaluation and critical thinking/ask students to write essays under timed conditions.

Do the graphs/charts provide you with useful information?

(*Duty: considering if visuals improve comprehension.*)

Visuals are clear and are referred to explicitly in the text. They help to improve comprehension of the issues.

What do you think is the best way to deal with students who plagiarise?

(*Duty: discussion question.*)

Group 2: *Summariser*

How does the title of the text relate to the content?

(*Duty: predicting content.*)

How is the text organised?

(*Duty: understanding organisation.*)

Students may pick up on the fact that there is an abstract, introduction, and that the main body of the article is divided into sections with headings. There are citations and a reference list at the end.

If you had to explain the main points in a clear and simple way to someone who hadn't read the text, what would you say?

(*Duty: summarising main points.*)

Group 3: *Highlighter*

While reading, highlight any vocabulary that is related to the topic of plagiarism (key terms).

(Duty: topical vocabulary.)

'Keywords' are highlighted at the start of the article, but others may include 'collusion', 'academic misbehaviour', 'gender bias'...

Are there any useful definitions given?

(Duty: finding useful definitions.)

There is a discussion of what the term 'plagiarism' means in section 1.1.

Is the style of the article informal, neutral, formal?

(Duty: style of language.)

This may be difficult for students to decide at present, but they may notice that it is more formal than spoken English or the 'narrative' style of English they may be used to from school essays.

Group 4: *Contextualiser*

Who is/are the author/authors? What do we know about them?

(Duty: learn more about authors to be able to recognise bias.)

Ask students to 'Google' the authors to see their backgrounds and if they have written anything else.

When/where does the text take place?

(Duty: place text into its broader context.)

Written in 2004 in the UK.

Is there any event/place mentioned in the text that it might be useful to learn more about?

(Duty: learn more about specific people, places, or events that the author mentions as support for points.)

Group 5: *Connector*

Can you make any connections with the content of the text and any personal experiences?

(Duty: make connections to personal experiences.)

Can you make any connections with this text and other texts you have read on the same or similar topics?

(Duty: make connections to content of the course, other readings, or subjects studied.)

Students will most likely not have read anything else on this, but they have seen the university website with advice on plagiarism and carried out the 'academic integrity' test, so they should be able to make connections with those.

Can you make any connections to current news or events?

(Duty: make connections to current news and events.)

Task 3

Purpose:

Suggested procedure: *Give small groups or partners one set of questions. Theirs do not have ARC roles listed on them. Ask them to talk about their answers to the questions together. After a reasonable time, have groups discuss the next set of questions. After they have all been done, ask groups to look at the questions and consider:*

- What kinds of things were the questions in each group asking?
- What aspect of the text do the questions seem to be focusing on?
- What have you learnt from this text about academic texts in general?

Task 4

Write a short reflection on this introduction to academic reading circles. Think about the following:

- What information did you learn from the text when you read it for the first time?
- After reading the different groups of questions, what else did you learn?

Presentations

Presentations are another fairly common type of assessment, and are utilised not only in university, but in various workplace settings. These can be group presentations or individual ones. The reasons for using group tasks have already been touched on earlier in this chapter, but, since our IFY students do a group seminar assessment, the presentation *we* ask them to do is an individual one. This means we are not over-assessing collaborative work and also allows each student to focus specifically on their chosen degree area in preparation for the transition onto their degree programme. They are asked to conduct independent research in order to present on a recent innovation (particularly suitable for engineering and business topics), a controversial issue (this is suitable for law, education, or healthcare subject areas), or an application of this subject to daily life (this encompasses subjects such as maths).

Abstracts

Alongside the presentation, students are required to write an abstract, which is assessed on its merits for a conference proposal. Again, writing an abstract forms the first part of making a presentation. If your proposal is not accepted, you won't need to make a PPT or deliver your presentation. So, asking students to write an abstract for an imaginary undergraduate conference is an 'authentic' task, or at least close to it.

You can see an example of the marking rubric for this assessment task in Chapter 5 of this guide. Again, as with all assessments, students need to be introduced to the genre of abstract writing and their skills, competencies, and language developed through a series of input sessions in class. And, since abstracts are also required for academic articles, this is another context for transferability.

If you are teaching on an IFY programme that stipulates assessment types, questions, and materials, the assessments described in this section could be used as formative assessments instead of summative ones. We are not suggesting that the assessment types we have focused on in this guide are the 'right' ones for all contexts.

The balance of the four skills

In our Language Centre, we are now starting to experiment with listening circles. These will operate in the same way as reading circles except that the texts will be oral rather than written. The challenge for tutors/materials writers here will be to find suitable listening texts as these are less common than written texts. The idea behind the introduction of listening circles is so that listening skills and competencies receive similar attention to reading skills and competencies, given that learners need good levels of both receptive skills before they can produce a high standard of productive work. In other words, writing and speaking assessment tasks in an academic context are almost always based on the use of information from sources.

It is generally accepted that attention is given to writing as this is often the 'product' in traditional summative assessments, but this is beginning to change. Therefore, we believe that to focus on writing and speaking at the expense of reading and listening would be disadvantageous to your IFY learners. As we have said, participation in speaking sessions is often an issue, with students from the Far East in particular. We know that any reluctance or reticence on a student's part can be the result of a multitude of factors, such as the broader educational context of previous study, the social and political environment, as well as individual perceptions of their own limitations, abilities, and personality traits, but, if you want to assist your students in gaining the most from their experience of international study, you will need to develop their confidence and encourage them to speak. And, in order to do that, they must develop their listening skills and competencies alongside speaking skills and competencies because a significant element of any group discussion or seminar is about *responding appropriately* to what has already been said. Features such as responding to the speaker's comments, inviting others to contribute, to expand or clarify on a point made or to develop the discussion by introducing a new point are just some of the reasons why 'good' active listening is necessary and these are the type of functions and features to consider, not only in the designing of assessments but also for learning and development through input and practice.

The impact of Covid-19 on assessment

The pandemic that began in 2020 had an immediate and significant impact on teaching, learning, and assessment practices. In the university, all teaching, learning, and assessment activities had to be transferred to an online mode of delivery with, of course, no prior warning. This had a dramatic impact on how assessments could be undertaken, overseen, and marked. The result was that, locally, different solutions were found, but, globally, there were rapid increases in academic integrity cases. This seemed to result from students either consciously or unconsciously resorting to external assistance with summative assessments. For example, there are companies known as 'content sharing' sites that target their marketing towards students, advertising through social media, infiltrating students' working groups and WhatsApp groups, and encouraging them to seek 'help' from their services. This can look very legitimate, but is in fact often the darker underbelly of the world of education with some of these companies blackmailing students if they don't pay or asking them for further monies for services provided. They have been known to report students for academic integrity breaches if students refuse to pay up and, in exchange for supplying answers to students' assessment questions, they demand the names of more of the student's peer group. In this way, it acts as a kind of pyramid selling where more and more students are hooked in.

At the time of writing, the decision made by our university is that the default for all assessments is that they should be online, but whether and to what extent that will continue remains unknown. It is likely, however, that at least some of the effects of Covid-19 will be long-lasting and the challenge for testing and assessment writers and administrators is likely to be how to balance assessment security with assessment inclusivity. We are becoming increasingly familiar with terms such as 'digital poverty', 'digital literacy', and 'remote proctoring', 'screen fatigue', 'sensitive camera use', each bringing with them a plethora of different and often opposing things to think about in connection with assessment. There are currently debates about whether remote proctoring tools are an invasion of privacy and do such tools wrongly assume that all students cheat? Does deploying such tools send the wrong message to students and thereby inadvertently encourage them to find ways to cheat? Should we instead start from a point of trust? Consult Dawson (2020) for an interesting look at what makes students feel compelled to use contract cheating services. But what is fair and equal for all? Bandwidths, connection speeds, equipment age and capability, access to sites such as YouTube or TED talks etc., can all vary. How does one balance validity and security in a digital assessment world?

There are an increasing number of voices in HE education calling for the days of the arguably archaic, sports hall type venue, three-hour written exams to be exchanged for more meaningful, real-world assessment tasks, which people in the workplace in a particular discipline would actually need to carry out. The hope is that this would both engage test takers in actively participating in learning and at the same time deter cheating. One thing that is clear is that students need very clear guidelines and instructions. For example, if they are not allowed to access sources other than the ones supplied to them, they need to know this. Can they use translation software? Online dictionaries? Should there be a requirement for cameras to be switched on for oral assessments? All the time? Some of the time? Can students use notes? Can they read from a script? Can an online presentation be considered as the same genre as a live presentation? Should oral assessments be live or pre-recorded? What constitutes audience engagement if there is no audience present? Setting clear boundaries and expectations will go some way to redressing the balance, but new ways of assessing student performance are also likely to continue to evolve.

Reflective team task

Now you are at the end of this chapter, here are some questions for you and your team to discuss together:

- How do you feel about using constructive alignment as a guiding approach to the way you think about joining up all the main building blocks of your course?
- How comfortable do you feel about analysing formative and summative assessments in order to ensure that the appropriate skills,

- competencies, and language washback into your teaching, input, and materials?
- Would you say you have the necessary skills and confidence to know how to scaffold student's learning? If not, what might you do to change this?
- Do you agree which points and how much more or how much less recycling might be necessary for specific skills, competencies, language items? (e.g. the mechanics of a referencing system or the use of information from sources in student's writing or speaking assignments.)
- To what extent do you think marking rubric need to be written for students to understand?
- Can you think of any ways in which you could maximise engagement with marking rubric and/or samples?
- How useful do you think it is to use exemplars with students?
- How do you personally respond to feedback? Is your answer different in a professional vs a personal context? Why is this?
- Does how you feel about receiving feedback affect your approach giving feedback to students? If so, in what way and should your feelings influence your practices?
- At which point(s) in the learning process do you feel feedback is most useful?
- What do you think about the idea of feedback being separate from assessment?
- Do you have any ideas about how you might use feedback in innovative ways?

References

BALEAP. 2008. *Competency Framework for Teachers of English for Academic Purposes*. [Online]. [Accessed 16 January 2019]. Available from: www.baleap.org/wp-content/uploads/2016/04/teap-competency-framework.pdf

Biggs, J. 1996. Enhancing Teaching through Constructive Alignment. *Higher Education*, **32** (3), pp347–364.

Biggs, J. and Tang, C. 2007. T*eaching for Quality Learning at University: What the Student Does*. 3rd edition. Maidenhead: McGraw Hill.

Biggs J. and Tang C. 2010. Applying Constructive Alignment to Outcomes-based Teaching and Learning, Training Material for "Quality Teaching for Learning in Higher Education" Workshop for Master Trainers, Ministry of Higher Education, Kuala Lumpur, 23–25 February 2010. [Online]. [Accessed 28 July 2021]. Available from: https://teaching.yale-nus.edu.sg/wp-content/uploads/sites/25/2017/03/biggs.tang_.constructive.alignment.What-is-CA-biggs-tang.pdf

Cambridge Assessment International Education. [no date]. *Getting Started with Assessment for Learning*. [Online]. [Accessed 28 July 2021]. Available from: www.cambridge-community.org.uk/professional-development/

Charles, M. and Pecorari, D. 2016. *Introducing English for Academic Purposes*. Oxon and New York: Routledge.

Cottrell, S. 2001. *Teaching Study Skills and Supporting Learning*. Basingstoke: Palgrave.

Dawson, P. 2020. *Defending Assessment against e-cheating: Design and Standards*. [Online]. [Accessed 30 November 2020]. Available from: https://au.bbcollab.com/collab/ui/session/playback

de Chazal, E. 2014. *English for Academic Purposes*. China: Oxford University Press.

Hübner, A. 2000. Assessment and accreditation of languages: implications for tutor training. In Hübner, A. Ibarz, T., and Laviosa. eds. *Assessment and Accreditation for Languages: The Emerging Consensus?* London: C*i*LT, pp81–102.

Manning, A. 2016. *Assessing EAP Theory and Practice in Assessment Literacy*. Reading: Garnet.

McKinley, J. and Thompson, G. 2018. Washback Effect in Teaching English as an International Language. [Online]. *TESOL Encyclopaedia of English Language Teaching*. [Accessed 28 July 2021]. Available from: www.englishappliedlinguistics.com/uploads/2/4/1/9/2419477/washback_effect_in_teaching_english_as_an_international_language_author_version.pdf

Moon, J. 2002. *The Module and Programme Development Handbook*. London: Kogan Page Limited.

Pinard, L. 2015. IATEFL 2015: Academic Reading Circles – Tyson Seburn. 12 April 2014. *Lizzie Pinard. Reflections of an English Language Teacher*. [Online]. [Accessed 15 July 2021]. Available from: https://reflectiveteachingreflectivelearning.com/2015/04/12/iatefl-2015-academic-reading-circles-tyson-seburn/

Seburn, T. 2015, *Academic Reading Circles*. Toronto: The Round.

The Bell Foundation. 2021. *Great Idea: Scaffolding. What is Scaffolding?* [Online]. [Accessed 28 July 2021]. Available from: www.bell-foundation.org.uk/eal-programme/guidance/effective-teaching-of-eal-learners/great-ideas/scaffolding/

Winstone, N. 2017. *High impact feedback: Engaging students as proactive recipients of feedback information*. [PowerPoint presentation]. HEA STEM Conference. 1–2 February. University of Surrey.

5 Managing IFY

Relevant BALEAP competencies:

Academic contexts:
1. *An EAP teacher will have a reasonable knowledge of the organizational, educational and communicative policies, practices, values and conventions of universities.*

Teaching practices:
10. *An EAP teacher will be familiar with the methods, practices and techniques of communicative language teaching and be able to locate these within an academic context and relate them to teaching the language and skills required by academic tasks and processes.*

(BALEAP, 2008)

Managing staff

Working together: Building a team

Finding the delicate balance between giving everyone a voice and managing them is the key to a happy team. Clearly, there are many variables to take into consideration in deciding on your approach to team building. It will depend, to some extent, on whether or not the individual team members have had experience of teaching EAP before and whether that has included any previous IFY teaching. Even if your teachers have taught EAP/IFY before, if this was in a different institution, it is likely that the philosophy and approach varied at least to some degree. Therefore, you cannot assume that all your teachers are working from a shared understanding. It will be up to you to make your approach crystal clear and to develop this shared understanding in some or all the following ways, as appropriate for the mix of staff on your team.

DOI: 10.4324/9781003253624-5

Individuals in your team

Think about each team member in terms of their age and experience, but also what strengths and weaknesses each person may bring into the team. This will help you not only to determine how much support each teacher might need but also who you can rely on in terms of delegating specific tasks to. Playing to people's strengths helps them to contribute more and therefore to feel valuable and valued, as well as giving you a much-needed hand. For example, is anyone on your team particularly interested in or adept at using new technology? If you are not, this person can be an invaluable time-saver for you at critical stages of the course.

Whatever your own strengths and weaknesses are, you will benefit from having a second pair of eyes on things. In our experience, no matter how many times you check your materials and messages, something will slip through the net. So, having a proof-reader on your team will help to catch those niggly details that must be correct but somehow aren't, such as dates where the day and date don't match or there are contradictory deadline times for submission in different documents. The pedant on your team who always notices spelling mistakes, missing commas, and other small details is a gift to you. So, rather than perhaps feeling frustrated with them, you should embrace their ability to spot all these things and, in doing so, they will probably feel a great sense of satisfaction too.

Resistance

It is worth bearing in mind that sometimes staff members are delegated to a teaching programme they are resistant to. This can make your life as a team manager more difficult, and you will need to think of ways you might be able to bring this person on side. Some suggestions will follow in this section of the guide, which you may find useful.

Setting deadlines

Some teachers are poor at admin or poor at meeting deadlines (or both). Whether or not this is the case with anyone on your team, you will still need to set very clear, realistic deadlines *well in advance* so that you don't put undue pressure on your teachers, and so that there are no excuses for not being aware of upcoming deadlines.

For example, if you have assessed presentations, you might want to pair teachers so that they can assess together. Before the assessment day, allow them a fixed amount of time to decide their groups' slots and then to put their schedule into a shared space; so that you can arrange cover easily should anyone be absent on the assessment day.

Minuted team meetings

Holding regular meetings, where minutes are taken and circulated to the team, are ways of getting your messages across to everyone in both oral and written forms (belt and braces approach). In that way, teachers can ask questions about anything they are not clear on in a face-to-face context and/or they can remind themselves of important things by reading the minutes as many times as they need to. Writing things down also provides evidence of what was said or agreed, should it be needed. Despite implementing these safety valves, it's still always best to assume that not everyone will be on the same page.

Never assume

You can't assume that everyone will read the minutes, your emails, or any other important document. Even if they do, it's amazing how many ways the same information can be interpreted. You will need to check regularly to make sure that your team are all on track, and that they stay that way. Don't assume that everyone is doing what is required simply because you have said it. This means checking regularly that your teachers are completing things as necessary. It will probably be too late to sort out problems at the end of the semester or the end of the year. You will also need to be prepared to *gently remind* your teachers to do what needs to be done in a timely manner, if anyone is falling behind. We find that sometimes a generic email is sufficient to nudge those who need it, but, at other times, you may need to communicate directly with an individual either remotely or face to face.

Offer support

As with students, it's always best to approach these things with sensitivity and to keep in mind that there could be underlying reasons why a member of your team is not performing to their full capacity or potential. This could be due to work-related issues or perhaps family life. Again, as with students, you need to be prepared to offer help and support where needed and agree together what form it is most appropriate for that to take.

Remember, too, that some things are above your pay grade, so, for example, if you have an underperforming teacher, it's not your job to deal with that. Pass it on to the right person in your organisation.

Renegades

Some extrovert, super-confident personality types can be difficult to manage; especially if they think they know better than you how things should be run/ done. You will need to keep an eye out for your more 'creative' teachers and you

94 *Managing IFY*

will need to be able to spot the renegade teacher who 'goes off piste' (perhaps despite your best efforts). Such teachers might not be teaching to the syllabus and, therefore, potentially disadvantaging their group in some way, but also, if they are away for any reason, it can be really tricky to cover their classes. They may not be in the same place as the other groups and you really need to know this in advance, so that whoever is covering the class is forewarned.

Keeping records of work

One way of trying to keep track of where each teacher is at is by asking your teachers to complete a record of work and gently reminding them to keep this up to date at regular intervals. You may also want to check records of work intermittently so that you can see for yourself that these are up to date. It's too late to discover that a teacher hasn't been filling them in when they are off work ill, as they may not be fit to tell you where they are up to with their teaching at that point. It also provides a record for external parties who may wish to check consistency, such as External Examiners or Inspection teams from BALEAP or the British Council (BC).

Fear of the unknown

Sometimes a lack of confidence can reveal itself as aggression. This can be a symptom of feeling overwhelmed or out of one's depth. So, if you feel under attack from one or more members of your team, it is worth keeping this in mind and trying to find the root of the problem rather than getting into conflict them with. For example, does the individual need more support to understand an assignment task? Would talking through things/explaining rationales help? Might a mentor or buddy help here? Or, would more documentation of some kind assist in clearing up any doubts in their mind? Might a checklist or a step-by step guide help? Sometimes teachers might fear loss of face or status if they openly admit they are experiencing some kind of difficulty, but a checklist or other written form of feedback might feel less threatening. Here is an example of one you might use or adapt:

Do you feel that you are getting sufficient support? Yes ☐ No ☐

If you answered no, in what areas do you need more support? Tick all that apply.
I need more help with:

Understanding the content of specific reading texts/lectures	☐
Understanding what the assessment title means	☐
Understanding specific academic requirements	☐
Managing the group	☐
Managing individual students	☐
Interpreting assessment rubric	☐
Marking using assessment rubric	☐
Working as team	☐
Working with specific team members	☐
Working autonomously	☐

Please give more detail for each of the areas you have ticked above:
What kind of support do you think would help you?
Discussion with the team ☐
Individual meetings with a specific person or people ☐
Extra reading ☐
Observation ☐
Other (please state) ☐
Please supply additional information about what you need and how often you might need this.

Another idea you might want to suggest to your new teachers is to write a reflective journal. This is often a good, non-threatening way of debriefing. You might want to read more about Kolb's Learning/Reflective Cycle (1975, 1984, cited in Manning, 2016) and the place of 'concrete experience', reflection, and experimentation in the cycle of developing practice.

Whether or not you will look at your teachers' reflective journals will possibly change the nature and honesty of their accounts. So, think carefully about whether or not you should be involved in this part of the process or whether it is a *self*-analysis, which may lead to the individual identifying they need more help. A different process would then be deployed for them to seek more help. You also need to be mindful of your teachers' workloads. Each additional thing you make compulsory has time implications, so think about how practical and how necessary each one might be before you make it a requirement.

Team composition

Once you have thought about your team as individuals, you will then need to think of them as a group. All groups have their own dynamics depending on any number of variables such as age, experience, gender, ethnicity, and personality. As with groups of students, you will need to work out where any friction might occur. Think carefully about who might not work well with whom when pairing or grouping staff for any particular tasks and activities in order to try to avoid pressure points. The larger the team, the more likely it is that differences and difficulties will occur, so thinking ahead about these things might help to prevent discord within your team. However, small teams can have their challenges too. It's best if you are in harmony about your approach to teaching, learning, and assessment as otherwise it can be very difficult to get anything done. Who is on your team may not be in your control, though, so establishing the non-negotiables might be wisest done early on as you may find this more difficult later, once habits have formed. Personality types can impact more significantly on small teams. If it's just two of you, for example, and you really don't see eye to eye, you will need to sit down and establish some ground rules for a smoother working relationship.

Pairing teachers in your team

Most often in our context, teachers work in pairs for assessment purposes. This is in order to address quality assurance and the reliability of assessment, an important feature of a rigorous assessment, by attempting to make marking consistent and an accurate reflection of the student's abilities (Charles and Pecorari, 2016).

Working in pairs might involve two teachers working together in the same room in order to assess oral assignments or remotely for the purpose of second/check marking of written scripts. Arguably, assessment can be an area that brings out teacher insecurity more than teaching so pairing staff might help to alleviate any such concerns. However, it might also have the reverse affect. Once again, as with student groups, you will need to consider your pairings quite carefully. It might be tempting to pair a quiet or new teacher with a more vocal or more experienced teacher. However, this kind of pairing can have its disadvantages for the newer or quieter member of the team in 'being heard'.

So, for example, you might want to pair two quieter members of your team together so that neither of them is shouted down in any grading 'discussions'. However, be aware that, if you also pair two vociferous people together, you will need to pre-empt any possible issues between them.

Whichever way you decide to pair your staff, try to avoid conflict between them by being clear that grading discussions must centre on the descriptors in the rubric and the assessment task, not who shouts the loudest getting their way with the final grade. Having clear rubric, clear task instructions, and clear processes and procedures for each assessment should help diffuse some of the tension of assessment times, by serving as a written reminder of exactly what they are looking for.

Mentoring/buddying systems

Here we are using the word 'mentor' loosely. We are simply referring to any informal pairing of members of staff for purely developmental purposes. Implementing such systems for staff to work together is one way of building an individual teacher's confidence in a specific area and can also be a way of developing shared understanding between your team members.

Equality

However, as with any other pairing or grouping, you will need to consider the points raised above in order to find suitable partnerships. For example, if you pair yourself with a new member of staff, you will need to be clear that the arrangement is purely developmental and not hierarchical. Development shouldn't be linked to any type of probation or assessment of the individual's performance. The mentee will need to be confident about expressing a lack of knowledge or understanding without fear of judgement or consequences to their employment or career advancement. Just because you think of yourself as being equal doesn't mean your mentee will see it that way. They might feel they have to accept you as a mentor even if they don't feel entirely comfortable, so wherever possible try to offer the mentee a choice of at least two potential mentors to choose from. Perhaps doing this remotely rather than face to face might allow for more honesty in the process.

Reciprocity

Any such informal mentoring or buddying arrangements may be reciprocal, with each party gaining something from the partnership. However, it could also be non-reciprocal, with only one party gaining something from the arrangement. It is also possible that individuals may be a mentee of one person in one capacity and a mentor of another in a different capacity. For example, I might be a mentee in the context of learning about Excel spreadsheets, but a mentor for someone embarking on a scholarship project. Whether or not the 'expert' on Excel is the same person as the one wishing to learn how to go about conducting scholarship, and whether or not all parties are at the same pay grade or level, is irrelevant as long they are all *comfortable* with their 'buddy' when they are in the position of mentee.

Staff new to EAP/IFY

As we have stated in other sections, it is likely that any teachers coming from an EFL background in particular will be on a steep learning curve the first time they teach on an EAP course (de Chazal, 2014; Hübner, 2000; Schmitt and Hamp-Lyons, 2015), which you can read more about in the forward to this guide. The focus of EAP teaching is centred on the cumulative acquisition of skills and academic language, the place, importance, and level of content in EAP classes, and the teacher taking on the role of assessor, are features likely to be unfamiliar to the 'new' IFY teacher. Therefore, they are likely to need more support in order to develop a clear understanding of what EAP teaching is in your institution/on your particular IFY course, as discussed above, and a buddy or mentoring system can be invaluable to reinforce these messages for such members of your team.

Demands placed on teachers

Although it is likely that as EFL teachers they will have encountered pressure for students to pass exams (perhaps IELTS in particular), these are normally externally devised and graded tests in which teachers are not directly involved as assessors. Therefore, in our experience, when coming on to IFY, 'new' teachers, even those with previous EAP teaching experience, can be intimidated or even overwhelmed by the demands placed upon them both in terms of the course content and delivery and the pressure of determining their students' futures through their role as assessor.

IFY modules, in our institution certainly, are particularly demanding on teachers in terms of getting the assessment 'right'. The IFY modules are credit bearing, and, therefore, high stakes courses where the difference between students going on to study their chosen degree depends exclusively on their performance on IFY and ultimately rests on their final grade(s). This, in our case, is different from our other provision such as pre-sessionals, where students merely have to 'successfully complete' their course in order to proceed onto their Master's programme, with no pass/fail element to the course. Therefore, marking and grading students' work can cause teachers some stress and anxiety. This, according to Schmitt and Hamp-Lyons (2015) is because EAP tutors are often not 'assessment literate'.

You might find it interesting to read some of the comments made by EAP practitioners in Manning (2016, pp183–185), as it may give you some insight into how teachers think and feel about their role as assessors.

As we have said previously, assessment has a central role in IFY provision. Therefore, it is essential that assessments are both valid and reliable (Schmitt and Hamp-Lyons, 2015). In order to be valid, they must measure ability in specified learning outcomes (Charles and Pecorari, 2016). Reliability, as we have said, is partly about consistency between markers and assessors. Charles and Pecorari (2016, p171) suggest that reliability can be affected by having different teachers teaching on a course over time and that a 'shared set of standards are needed' in order to avoid this. In an ideal world, you would have a mature, established team who all share the same values and standards, but the reality is often very different. This is yet another reason why it is essential to have clear and explicit rubric, guidelines, and assessment tasks for teachers to work with.

Managing assessment

Myth busting with teachers

It is worth coming back to the point raised earlier that, generally, as EFL/EAP teachers we traditionally have not received any specific training or gained any qualifications as markers or examiners. Although Hübner noted this in 2000, Schmitt and Hamp-Lyons make the same point in 2015. Manning, in 2016, also suggests that these are still amongst a range of *assumed skills* that sit alongside classroom teaching. He suggests that there has been 'a lack of prominence attributed to the process of assessment in teacher education courses' (Brindley, 2008, cited in Manning, 2016, p74) as do Schmitt and Hamp-Lyons (2015), and this situation has given rise to much debate around the idea of teachers and their assessment literacy. We have personally seen the results of the lack of uniformity in the different ways in which teachers can approach marking.

Some teachers are much more assessment literate and understand the importance of standardised, transparent assessment, while others seem not to take it seriously and instead approach assessment in more ad hoc, random ways. There are EAP teachers who focus their assessment primarily on language at the expense of skills and important features of academic work. They admit that this is because they feel more comfortable assessing language than content or use of sources. Therefore, such assessors can, perhaps, be thought of as being partially literate. Our experience is therefore contrary to de Chazal (2014) who suggests that teachers working in EAP have a cohesive view of what EAP is. All in all, the implications are that meeting BALEAP descriptor 11: 'the EAP teacher will be able to assess academic language and skills using formative and summative assessment' (BALEAP, 2008, p9) may require much more work for those new to in-house assessment than it may first appear, no matter how many years they have been teaching.

As previously mentioned, assessing student performance through in-house assessments and examinations is particularly prevalent in the UK university context, with IFY programmes being high stakes in terms of students having to meet the necessary grades for entry onto their chosen degrees (Schmitt and Hamp-Lyons, 2015). Therefore, this generally means that teachers will need to acquire a new set of skills in order to meet the demands of markers or assessors. This can be daunting for some teachers and may even be demotivating (Brown and Bailey, 2008, cited in Manning, 2016). As a result, it is important that assessment tasks and assessment systems are transparent and rigorous in order to provide sufficient help and support to the 'new' assessors on their journey to becoming fully assessment literate as much as to aid consistency between markers.

Through objectivity

As we have said earlier, assessments such as essays and presentations are subjective rather than cloze tests or discrete item testing, which are objective. Objective tests can be marked by machines as they require no interpretation and have right or wrong answers. However, as we have discussed, subjectivity can also mean focusing on one feature more than another in the assessment of student performance, for example, language over skills. This form of subjectivity can pose another threat to reliability (Charles and Pecorari, 2016) because teachers may mark more harshly or more leniently as a result.

As the successful completion of IFY modules are often so pivotal in determining the future direction of a student's life, teachers may sometimes be tempted to make emotional decisions or allow themselves to be pressured by students to award the required marks irrespective of the student's actual performance in the task/ability. Sometimes teachers may take into account the effort or progress student X has made, despite the odds perhaps, or make a judgement about how well student Y will be able to cope in their department and on their chosen degree course. These, however, are not factors that should be taken into account. In criterion-referenced assessments, only the performance of the student at the time of the assessment is measured against the descriptors for those specific criteria. (If you would like to read more on this, Manning (2016) talks about it in chapter 7 of his book).

However, as Keating (2019) points out, where marking is subjective there is always likely to be more disparity between markers than in objective marking. That is because answers are not simply right or wrong and the qualitative elements are not entirely judgement free. Keating (2019) also states that 'exam boards and their markers should work hard to narrow the range of plausible marks, through good mark schemes and good examiner training'. In this case, the exam board is the in-house assessment team and it therefore falls to course managers to strive for as much parity and equity between markers as possible. By ensuring that teachers are marking from the rubric, and utilising the marking scheme appropriately, in conjunction with the specific task being assessed, subjective elements such as those mentioned above can, hopefully, be eliminated from assessment variables or at least be significantly minimised.

Through standardisation of your team

As a first step in tackling issues around perceptions of 'strict' or 'hard' markers vs 'soft' or 'lenient' markers, it is important that you, as the team leader, have confidence that your team members are all marking, more or less, to the same standard, within acceptable norms of variance. As we have touched on earlier, and Rhead and Black (2018) also suggest, consistency between markers varies according not only to whether the marking is objective or subjective, but is also according to subject area and there is less accuracy in essay-related marking (i.e. longer answers and subjective marking). If we look closely at the study by Ofqual (Rhead and Black, 2018) of different subject areas in relation to consistency of marking, we can see substantial variance in the percentages. It may also be the case that there are differences in what exam boards expect from their markers. However, for our marking purposes, consistency is considered achieved when markers are marking within three marks of one another. If there are more variances than you consider acceptable after getting all your team to mark the same sample(s), this may be because of the rubric.

If you have written your own rubric, the standardisation exercise may help you to identify any areas where changes need to be made. If, however, you are using external rubric, you will need to make decisions about how criteria and descriptors should be interpreted collectively.

The art of writing assessment rubric

It could be argued that criterion-referenced assessment is more reliable than norm referenced assessment, in terms of facilitating consistent, stable standards and it is certainly the case that criterion-referenced assessment is common practice in universities in the UK (deChazal, 2014). However, it is still important to remember that assessing is, arguably, an art form rather than a science. Therefore, there will always be an element of subjectivity involved in the process (Davies, 1990; Keating, 2019) despite Ofqual's latest research project looking into how effective training, standardisation, and moderation can be in aligning markers (Keating, 2019). This is because, whatever words you use to describe and differentiate different levels of performance, individual markers will always have to *interpret* them. However, our job as rubric writers and assessors is to make those subjective elements as small and negligible as possible.

Task-specific vs generic rubric

There are two distinct choices for rubric; one is task specific and the other is generic. In rubric written specifically for a task, the descriptors can be written to take into account the nuances of that particular task. So, for example, if you have a group presentation task, the various group elements of this task can be written into the descriptors. How the presentation flowed between presenters, the language they used to do this, the coherence of the content over all presentation not just each individual segment, are examples of group aspects of performance.

Here is an example:

Group oral presentation marking rubric

90–80	Group mark: Content	*No room for improvement:* An excellent and complete response to the task in terms of both content and organisation. The content is entirely relevant and highly appropriate for a non-specialist audience. There is very clear evidence of analysis as well as description demonstrating an in-depth understanding of the topic. The content demonstrates fully appropriate research and use of the company's website. There is excellent support to ideas as and where appropriate.
	Group mark: Organisation	Excellent organisation of content throughout (introduction and conclusion and staging of key points, development of ideas). Excellent use of time, and excellent balance between the contributions of each team member. Excellent links and transitions between team members. Excellent visual aids to support presentation, which are used very appropriately.
	Individual mark: Technique	Excellent presentation skills in terms of use of voice level, pacing body language, eye contact. Excellent attempt to interest the audience and to gain and establish contact. An excellent manner, confident and appropriately formal/professional. The speaker has the ability to keep the audience interested throughout.

	Individual mark: *Language*	Excellent clarity of message and intelligibility (pronunciation) at all times and easy for audience to make notes. Excellent use of language (grammar and vocabulary, presentation language), in terms of appropriacy and accuracy.
79–70	**Group mark:** *Content*	***There is little room for improvement:*** A very good and complete response to the task in terms of both content and organisation. The content is relevant and highly appropriate for a non-specialist audience. There is clear evidence of analysis as well as description demonstrating a solid understanding of the topic. The content demonstrates fully appropriate research and use of the company's website. There is very good support to ideas as and where appropriate.
	Group mark: *Organisation*	Very good organisation of content throughout (introduction and conclusion and staging of key points, development of ideas). Very good use of time and very good balance between the contributions of each team member. Very good links and transitions between team members. Very good visual aids to support presentation, which are used appropriately.
	Individual mark: *Technique*	Very good presentation skills in terms of use of voice level, pacing, body language, eye contact. Very good attempt to interest the audience and to gain and establish contact. A very good manner; confident and appropriately formal professional. The speaker has the ability to keep the audience interested throughout.
	Individual mark: *Language*	Very good clarity of message and intelligibility (pronunciation) at all times and easy for audience to make notes. Very good use of language (grammar and vocabulary, presentation language), in terms of appropriacy and accuracy.
69–60	**Group mark:** *Content*	***There is some room for improvement.*** A good response to the task overall, but may be stronger in one element than the other (in terms of content and organisation). The content is mostly relevant and appropriate for a non-specialist audience. There is evidence of analysis as well as description demonstrating an understanding of the topic, but there may be minor slips. The content demonstrates mostly appropriate research and use of the company's website. There is good support to ideas, which are generally used as and where appropriate.

	Group mark: *Organisation*	Good organisation of content throughout (introduction and conclusion and staging of key points, development of ideas). Good use of time, with a good balance between the contributions of each team member. Good links and transitions between team members. Good visual aids to support presentation, which are mainly used appropriately.
	Individual mark: *Technique*	Good presentation skills in terms of use of voice level, pacing, body language, eye contact. Good attempt to interest the audience and to gain and establish contact. A good manner; confident and formal/professional for the most part, but there may be minor slips. The speaker has the ability to keep the audience interested, but this may not be throughout the entire duration of their turn.
	Individual mark: *Language*	Good clarity of message and intelligibility (pronunciation) at all times and easy for audience to make notes. Good use of language (grammar and vocabulary, presentation language), in terms of appropriacy and accuracy.
59–50	**Group mark:** *Content*	*There is some room for improvement:* A satisfactory response to the task overall, but may be weaker in one element than the other (in terms of content and organisation). Some content is relevant and appropriate for a non-specialist audience. There is some evidence of analysis as well as description demonstrating an understanding of the topic, but there may be some slips. The content demonstrates adequate research and mostly appropriate use of the company's website. There is some support to ideas, but this may sometimes be used inappropriately.
	Group mark: *Organisation*	Adequate organisation of content throughout (introduction and conclusion and staging of key points, development of ideas). Adequate use of time, with some attempt at balance between the contributions of each team member. Some attempt at links and transitions between team members. Adequate visual aids to support presentation, which are used mostly appropriately.
	Individual mark: *Technique*	Adequate presentation skills in terms of use of voice level, pacing, body language, eye contact. Adequate attempt to interest the audience and to gain and establish contact. A satisfactory manner; may not be consistently confident and formal/professional. The speaker may not keep the audience interested throughout the entire duration of their turn.

	Individual mark: *Language*	Adequate clarity of message and intelligibility (pronunciation) at all times and possibility for audience to make notes. Adequate use of language (grammar and vocabulary, presentation language), in terms of appropriacy and accuracy.
49–40	**Group mark:** *Content*	***There is significant room for improvement:*** A poor response to the task overall. One element may be significantly weaker than the other (in terms of content and organisation). Only some of the content is relevant and/or appropriate for a non-specialist audience. There is little evidence of analysis and the presentation is mostly descriptive, demonstrating limited understanding of the topic. The content demonstrates little evidence of research and use of the company's website may not be appropriate. There is little support to ideas and any support offered may be inappropriate.
	Group mark: *Organisation*	Poor organisation of content throughout (introduction and conclusion and staging of key points, development of ideas). Poor use of time, most probably with a lack of balance between the contributions of each team member. Few attempts at links and transitions between team members. Poor visual aids to support presentation, which are not used appropriately.
	Individual mark: *Technique*	Poor presentation skills in terms of use of voice level, pacing, body language, eye contact. Poor attempt to interest the audience and to gain and establish contact, and the content is appropriate for a non-specialist audience. An unsatisfactory manner; may not be consistently confident and/or sufficiently formal/professional. The speaker may only keep the audience interested in isolated parts of their turn.
	Individual mark: *Language*	Poor clarity of message and intelligibility (pronunciation) at all times and difficult for audience to make notes. Poor use of language (grammar and vocabulary, presentation language), in terms of appropriacy and accuracy.
39–30	**Group mark:** *Content*	***This is an unsatisfactory performance:*** A very poor response to the task overall. Both elements of the task may be weak (in terms of content and organisation). Very little content is relevant and/or appropriate for a non-specialist audience. There is very little or no evidence of analysis and the presentation may be entirely descriptive, demonstrating very little understanding of the topic. The content demonstrates very little evidence of research and use of the company's website may not be appropriate (or it may not have been used). There is very little or no support to ideas and/or any support that is offered may be inappropriate.

	Group mark: *Organisation*	Inadequate organisation of content throughout (introduction and conclusion and staging of key points, development of ideas).
		Inadequate use of time, with no balance between the contributions of each team member.
		No attempt at links and transitions between team members.
		Visual aids may not support the presentation.
	Individual mark: *Language*	Poor clarity of message and intelligibility (pronunciation) at all times and very difficult for audience to make notes.
		Poor use of language (grammar and vocabulary, presentation language), in terms of appropriacy and accuracy.
29–20	**Group mark:** *Content*	*This is a very unsatisfactory performance:* Little or no attempt at a response to the task overall.
		Both the content and organisation of the presentation are inadequate/ inappropriate.
		Very little or none of the content is relevant and/or appropriate for a non-specialist audience.
		There is no evidence of analysis and the presentation is entirely descriptive, demonstrating very no understanding of the topic.
		The content demonstrates very little to no evidence of research and use of the company's website may not be appropriate (or it may not have been used at all).
		There is very little or no support to ideas and/or any support that is offered may be inappropriate.
	Group mark: Organisation	Very inadequate organisation of content throughout (introduction and conclusion and staging of key points, development of ideas).
		Very inadequate use of time, with no balance between the contributions of each team member.
		No attempt at links and transitions between team members.
		Visual aids do not support the presentation.
	Individual mark: Technique	Very inadequate presentation skills in terms of use of voice level, pacing, body language, eye contact.
		Very inadequate attempt to interest the audience and to gain and establish contact, and the content is not appropriate for a non-specialist audience.
		A very unsatisfactory manner; may not be confident and/or sufficiently formal/professional.
		The speaker may not keep the audience interested at all.

The other choice is a generic set of rubric, which you use for every assessment on your course. Below is an example of everything 'pass' level and above.

106 *Managing IFY*

Language and Communication		80+	79–70	69–65	64–60	59–55 Standard Expected Level	54–50
Fluency and Cohesion	**Range of devices** **Accuracy** **Fluency**	Exceeds descriptors to an extent that can be described as 'outstanding'.	Accurately uses a sophisticated range of discourse markers to achieve a natural flow throughout. Slight hesitations may occur, but only when searching for ideas.	Accurately uses a wide range of discourse markers to very good effect throughout. Hesitations may occur, but these are mainly content related.	Uses a range of discourse markers to good effect. Few mistakes occur. There are very few hesitations when searching for language.	Uses a range of discourse markers generally to good effect. Some mistakes may occur. There may be occasional hesitation when searching for language, but no breakdowns in communication.	Uses a range of discourse markers; mistakes may lead to lack of clarity. Some hesitation may result in some small breakdowns in communication.
Grammar & Lexis	**Range** **Accuracy & Appropriacy**	Exceeds descriptors to an extent that can be described as 'outstanding'.	Uses a wide range of grammatical structures with total flexibility. Effective use of a wide range of lexis and discipline-specific language to convey very specific meaning. Paraphrases with ease if required. High level of accuracy with very few minor mistakes. The message is very clear throughout.	Uses a wide range of grammatical structures with flexibility. Effective use of a wide range of lexis and discipline specific language. Paraphrases with ease if required. High level of accuracy. There may be some minor or systematic mistakes, but the message is always clear.	Uses a range of grammatical structures with flexibility. Effective use of a range of lexis and discipline specific language. Paraphrases successfully. Language is well-controlled for accuracy. Some small mistakes may occur in complex language, but the message is clear.	Uses a range of grammatical structures with some flexibility. Some awareness of lexis and discipline-specific language. Attempts at paraphrasing are generally successful. Basic language is well-controlled for accuracy. Mistakes may occur in complex language, but the message is mostly clear.	Uses a range of grammatical structures with limited flexibility. Some awareness of commonly used lexis and discipline-specific language. Paraphrasing may be unclear. Frequent lack of accuracy in basic structures and some errors may affect the message.

		Exceeds / Outstanding				
Pronunciation	Word intelligibility / Use of stress / intonation / Pace	Exceeds descriptors to an extent that can be described as 'outstanding'.	Uses stress, intonation and pausing to communicate nuanced meaning. Intelligible throughout. Very few words mispronounced.	Uses stress, intonation, and pace very effectively. Intelligible throughout. Only minor mispronunciation of key words.	Uses stress, intonation, and pace effectively. Intelligible throughout. Occasional mispronunciation of key words, but message is still clear.	Attempts to use stress, intonation, and pace, with some success. There may be some mispronunciation of keywords, but the message is generally clear.	Limited attempts to use stress, intonation, and pace. Mispronounces some key words and the message is occasionally unclear.
Visual Communication	Audience engagement / Use of notes/ slides	Exceeds descriptors to an extent that can be described as 'outstanding'.	Uses eye contact and gesture very effectively. Maintains audience engagement in a very natural way. Slides are very clear and support the purpose of the presenter. There are no mistakes on the slides.	Uses eye contact and gesture very effectively. Maintains audience engagement confidently. Slides are very clear and support the purpose of the presenter. There may be some minor mistakes.	Good use of eye contact and gesture. Engages audience well. Slides are clear and support the purpose of the presenter. There are very few mistakes.	Some good use of eye contact and gesture. Generally engages the audience. Slides are mostly clear and support the purpose of the presenter. There may be some mistakes.	Attempts to use eye contact and gesture and to engage the audience, but not always with success. A few slides are unclear, maybe a little content heavy and/or the presenter may sometimes depend on them for support. There may be numerous mistakes.

Notes for use

The rubric are intended to be used for 'on-the-spot' assessment and to be formative for students, that is, they contain teachable language and can be used independently by students in self-assessment practice.

Task fulfilment is general so that it can be applied to different genres/task types. Further instructions and advice, that is, content-related guidelines for successful task completion, should be made available as an additional document online.

Timing is subsumed into Content and Organisation mark. Presentations that go over time should be stopped at the maximum time allowed. Presentations that have an imbalance of sections will also lose marks here.

Critical thinking is embedded in Organisation and Content / Use of Sources.

Communicative ability – '*negotiating meaning if required*' refers to the student's skills at the Q&A should any clarification of language and/or content be required. This part of the presentation should be well-planned and suitably timed in order to allow presenters sufficient opportunity to explain and clarify their knowledge.

Fluency & Cohesion:

- '*Uses a range of discourse markers*' refers to language use that 'signposts' discourse and manages flow and structure.
- '*Breakdowns in communication*' refers to extended hesitation (or overuse of connectives/fillers) that affect the message negatively.
- Over-dependence on memorised language that impedes delivery can be penalised in Fluency and Cohesion under '*breakdowns*', or marked down under Visual Communication '*engagement of audience*'.

Pronunciation:

- '*Attempts to use stress*' should **not** be interpreted as 'stress timing', but as use of stress on key words (nuclear or tonic stress) to draw attention to key points of interest/importance.
- '*Attempts to use pace*' includes effective pausing between utterances.

Assessment is weighted 50/50.

There are arguments for and against both of these options. With task-specific rubric it can be argued that the teacher might be overloaded and confused by all the different criteria and descriptors.

However, conversely, it can be said that task-specific rubric provide clarity and focuses directly on the detailed requirements of the task. With generic rubric, the arguments are made that they provide greater standardisation across all marking teams and courses. However, they may not always be as explicit or simple enough for the teacher to use as they may require more interpretation than task-specific rubric.

If you have the choice and you opt for generic rubric, it will probably still be necessary to have two generic sets; one for oral assessments and one for written, as the features of each of these skills are very different. If you adopt a generic-rubric approach the importance of using these alongside the task becomes yet more critical since there is more ambiguity and, therefore, more room for confusion when marking. This may be because the task being assessed does not have all of the requirements as they are laid out in the generic descriptors and staff are then not sure what they should do with these 'extra' descriptors. For example, if there are descriptors detailing critical engagement with the content, but the task is a descriptive task, then do markers assess criticality somehow or ignore this descriptor? In such cases, standardisation meetings will be crucial in ensuring that all teachers are using the rubric in the same way.

As indicated in Hübner's (2000) Assessment Principles 11, 12, and 13, the assessment task will need to include instructions to the students on how critical thinking will, or possibly will not, be assessed. Staff will then need to apply the task instructions to the rubric in order not to penalise the students for not doing something that they were not required to do by the task in the first place. This would fully encapsulate the BALEAP (2008, p9) competency describing the EAP teacher's 'ability to apply marking rubric consistently and to an agreed standard'.

An argument for the use of task-specific rubric

As you may have gathered from the commentary above, our preference is for task-specific rubric since we believe it can be another tool with which to assist in the standardisation of the team. Teacher feedback given to us is that having clear and appropriate descriptors for each task, without confusing anomalies, and the inclusion of an overarching strapline (see below for an explanation of straplines) for each band, helps them to orient themselves to the standard level expected of the students even when the assessor is new to the module. These features help to alleviate stress for the individual assessor and contribute to parity between more and less experienced members of the team. However, you may not be in a position to choose which rubric you adopt. In which case, you will need to find ways within the constraints you have of achieving the same aim.

Consistent and constructive wording of rubric

As we have said, one significant way of reducing subjectivity can be through writing 'good' rubric. So, if you are going to write your own, can be whether they are task-specific or generic, in order to minimise variation in the way teachers *interpret* the rubric it is important to be consistent in the use of language for and level of each band. For example, use words that are consistent in the same band. If you decide on the word 'excellent' for use in the top band, then use that same word or other words that are equal to it in each descriptor wherever it is appropriate in that same band. You may use 'very good' for the band below, 'good' for the next one down, and 'satisfactory' or 'adequate' for a low pass band.

See the example below, which is for the top band of a written report. You can see that the words underlined attempt to indicate the extent to which the descriptor needs to be achieved. The intensifiers such as 'very' and 'highly' are arguably redundant, and you may choose not to use them. However, how much differentiation you need to make between bands will depend on the number of bands you have altogether, and this number might be determined by your institution as ours are.

The actual wording you choose to describe performance will depend on whether or not your courses are pass/fail. In the case of automatic progression from, say, pre-sessional courses such as ours at Leeds, onto their chosen degree programmes, it would not be appropriate to describe the standards the students reach at the end as pass/fail. Whichever terminology you use, try to make it positive in the spirit of getting away from a deficit module of learning. Cottrell (2001, p40) talks about the importance of supportive learning environments and making learning a 'more constructive experience' for the learner and wording can also make a small contribution towards this. Using words such as 'poor' rather than 'approaching' (for levels below that of the standard required) can have a very different effect on the learner.

Sometimes less is more: Spot marking

If you have more flexibility, you might want to think carefully about reducing the number of bands to approaching standard (otherwise known as fail), standard expected (low pass/pass), or excellent (high pass/pass with merit).

However, some institutions require much more differentiation than others. So, you may find there are several bands; not just three or four. This also applies to marks within a band. The more marks there are in each band, the more difficult it can be to determine exactly which one is appropriate for the performance. Why, for example, give a 56 and not a 57? Or why award a 51 instead of a 52? Again, if you can be autonomous in making this decision, we suggest using only three marks within a band; low, middle, and high. The only marks possible in this scheme would be 2, 5, and 8. So, for example, assessors would mark a satisfactory performance at either 52, 55, or 58 depending on the other variables within that satisfactory performance band. This is known as 'spot marking' or 'categorical marking'. We, as you can see from our rubric, used the full range of numbers from 0–9 in our institution. However, we have now moved to spot marking in the Language Centre and, hopefully, the rest of the university will do the same at some point.

There are, of course, also other ways of marking, some without numeric values, such as the Common European Framework of Reference known as the CEFR (Council of Europe, 2021), which was designed to facilitate understanding of different qualifications within Europe.

The 'Grade Marking' project undertaken at Southampton Solent University (Handley and Read, 2016) makes for interesting reading as it details the change from a percentage-based marking scheme to a 17-point equivalent with letters and numbers. The paper highlights some of the difficulties in changing thinking at both a marker level and an institutional one.

Senge (cited in Handley and Read, 2016, no pagination) differentiates between compliance and commitment. The former being a 'superficial response to an initiative' and the latter one based on personal values and beliefs. Handley and Read (2016) were more interested in marker thinking and how that contributed to commitment. This differentiation in marker approach raises some interesting questions and gives food for thought about what impacts values and beliefs.

100–80	Content	Excellent selection of content. ***Student has written a report that responds to the task instructions <u>very appropriately</u> and all of the content is <u>highly relevant</u>.*** The objectives of the report are *very clear*. The executive summary contains *all* required information. Demonstrates *excellent* understanding of concept/issues covered in the project. The report includes a clear examination of the chosen aspect of health and a *very rational* and *coherent* evaluation of the health promotion activities undertaken. The reader can follow the report with *no effort*. There is an overall flow/sense of coherence. The report contains a *very logical* and appropriate conclusion. The links to the topic are *explicit* and *very clearly* explained.
	Secondary sources	Provides *sound evidence* to support writing. Makes *sophisticated* use of sources to support ideas. Student has conducted *highly relevant research* of their own, which is *entirely appropriate*. *Very accurate* referencing.
	Structure	*Very clear and logical* overall structure for a report. Content is divided into clearly structured sections and paragraphs. Headings and sub-headings are used *very effectively and accurately* reflect the content of each section. Content is linked together *very effectively*.

What you need to avoid when writing your rubric is using words/phrases that make lower bands sound more difficult to achieve than higher bands. For example, if you said 'sophisticated' use of sources in the pass band and 'good' use of sources in the high pass band that would send very confusing messages to both students and markers.

You also need to avoid using words/phrases that do not clearly differentiate between the levels of achievement in each band. For example, if you said 'highly effective' use of sources in the pass band and 'sophisticated' use of sources in the high pass band, it may not be clear which one requires more skill in using sources. The more you can avoid adjectives and adverbs the better.

Matching descriptors to the specific assessment task

As discussed above, you can begin to address standardisation of marking by writing a clear and transparent set of rubric that are relatively simple for teachers to use and, importantly, which match the task being assessed. For example, if the task does not require the student to *evaluate* anything, then, logically, the rubric or criteria must not include descriptors that refer to this. If the assessment is a group task, the criteria and descriptors in the rubric should be written to include 'group requirements' such as how a presentation flowed between the different speakers.

The use of straplines

As we have said, teachers are individuals and as such do not all automatically use rubric in the same way. Some teachers can be unsure of which band to place an assessment in if it exhibits different levels of achievement in the various bands. One tool we have developed over the years and have found useful is to use straplines in our rubric to help markers to determine the band. In the sample below, you can see the strapline '*the student has produced an abstract that ... would be acceptable for use in an undergraduate conference programme*'.

These are the straplines for bands below:

> *The student has produced an abstract that, with some minor alterations, would be acceptable for use in an undergraduate conference programme.*
> *The student has produced an abstract that would not be acceptable for use in an undergraduate conference programme without significant alterations.*
> *The student has produced a text that would not be acceptable in its current form for use in an undergraduate conference programme.*

The assessor reads the student's abstract and decides which strapline the piece of work best fits depending on whether there are any, some, or many alterations needed. This determines the band. Now that the marker has the band, they move the mark up or down in the band depending on how well the individual descriptors have been fulfilled, starting from the middle mark of the band (e.g. 55).

80–100	Excellent response to the task set. *The student has produced an abstract that would be acceptable for use in an undergraduate conference programme.*
	• The content of the abstract is extremely relevant and highly accessible for a non-specialist audience. Content is explicitly and clearly explained, and logically linked throughout.
	• The aim of the presentation is extremely clear and specific.
	• The four main elements expected in an abstract are present and clearly and easily identifiable using appropriate linguistic devices.
	• The four main elements and the aim appear in a logical sequence.
	• Extremely accurate use of grammar and vocabulary, and written in a highly appropriate semi-formal style.
	• An accurate reference list has been included.
	• Any source material used is paraphrased extremely well.
	• The word count has been used skilfully to write succinctly.

Including guidelines on how to use the rubric

Again, because assessors may forget how to use the rubric, or may not be sure but don't want to lose face by asking, we find it helpful to include guidelines at the end of each of the rubric. These provide a transparent, written record for students and assessors to see, and this is another tool you can think about adding to your standardisation arsenal. As you can see from the example we've included here, it is also important to state the overriding features of a piece of work that would determine its level. For us, these are task fulfilment and plagiarism, or other forms of malpractice.

Task fulfilment

Not all courses or providers view task fulfilment in the same way, so, again, it is important to make decisions about importance of the task in the marking scheme and to communicate these things to your team. For example, in some institutions it may be perfectly possible for a student to write an essay that is not on task, but this is accepted and marked in exactly the same way as another student's piece of work that is. In our opinion, this approach has two significant downsides:

Comparability

First, if a student is not answering the set question, why is it there in the first place? Students could simply be given a topic and allowed to write about that in any way they see fit. However, this poses its own problems because of the breadth and depth of all the different possible responses, and, therefore, they would be very difficult to view as the same task. That, presumably, is why assessments are generally given in the form of a specific question or questions rather than as topics. In order to measure comparability across a cohort, the title, surely, must be the key. The extent to which the student addresses the question should then predominately determine the band awarded. In other words, the extent to which the student *fulfils the task* they were given. Otherwise, if students write any content they want to yet still receive a high mark, this mark may not be worth the same as another student's high mark for writing something altogether different.

More opportunities for cheating

Second, if task fulfilment is not of primary importance, it can allow students a little more room to cheat. For example, in a situation where the students are in a timed writing or examination situation, if they don't answer the question as set on the paper it could be because they have memorised a piece of writing either they, or someone else, did beforehand and simply regurgitated it on the day. Similarly, we have found that, when students buy their assignments from essay mills or other students, we can immediately tell because these kinds of essays or reports do not quite hit the right note. They may be written in excellent English, which is a point we will discuss later, but they are usually a little bit too general in terms of the content and they do not directly and fully answer the question. They talk around it or answer a slightly different question. They do not use sources we have stipulated, or they claim in their reference list to have used hard copies of books, but yet there are no copies in our university library or they are very old, slightly odd choices of sources. So, what we are saying is that the question can sometimes catch out those who seek to cheat. This, with the growing issues around contract cheating sites and essay mills, in our minds, is sufficient reason which can make task fulfilment an overriding factor in determining the level of performance.

Determining what plagiarism is and isn't

Plagiarism is another aspect of academic work that, perhaps surprisingly, not everyone views in the same way. So, for the purpose of clarity, when we talk about plagiarism here we mean deliberate attempts to use the work of others without *any* form of acknowledgement.

This is different from the stance adopted in the university at large where any kind of poor referencing is viewed as a deliberate attempt to plagiarise. Our role as EAP teachers is to teach students how to reference and how to use sources in their work, but it is unreasonable to expect students not to make mistakes in these skills as they are learning them. Clearly, learning how to use a referencing system such as Harvard style is purely mechanical, which, with practice, students can become adept at. Therefore, if students make attempts at acknowledging their sources but use the first name instead of the family name of the author, include the entire website address instead of simply the name and date, or any other small slip of this kind we would think of that as *poor academic practice* rather than an attempt to plagiarise.

However, mechanical systems and their details aside, *using* the content from a source in their writing is much more complicated and requires mastery in a number of skills, such as synthesising, paraphrasing, summarising, before we even come on to the grammatical and lexical challenges of incorporating the information they find into their own sentences. Students often struggle with the extent to which they should use their own words and ideas vs the number of words and ideas they should take from sources as this is often something completely new to them. We tell them that they need to support their writing and use evidence, but, often, they are not sure how this should be done. All of this takes a lot of practice to get right. We believe that our primary role is to support students on their developmental journey. Therefore, we should focus on the formative elements even in their summative assessments and this approach would seem to fit into Hübner's (2000, pp81–102) Assessment Principles 3, 9, and 10. Namely that 'assessments should be an integral part of the learning process ... that assessment activities should be accompanied by well-presented support material and that they should be reinforced by constructive encouraging feedback'.

With this formative focus in mind, our definition of *plagiarism* is chunks of copied language or any content/ideas taken from a source without *any* attempt to acknowledge this or to include a citation or speech marks. Other forms of errors and mistakes in referencing or using information from sources are viewed as *poor academic practice*, otherwise known as patch writing. 'Patch writing involves "copying from a source text and then deleting some words, altering grammatical structures or plugging in one-for-one synonym-substitutes"' (Howard, 1993, p233 cited in Newton, Wright and Newton, 2014).

The extent to which either plagiarism or poor practice happens in any one piece of work will determine the severity of the case, but some form of penalty will be applied. These will be predetermined by your institution or course provider. You will need to find out what these policies, rules, and penalties are and apply them consistently. This falls into BALEAP competency framework descriptor '1: Academic contexts' that the EAP teacher will have 'reasonable knowledge of disciplinary procedures' (2008, p4).

A 'possible indicator' of the teacher's ability in this context might be that students 'use appropriate citation and referencing in learning activities and prepared assessment tasks' (BALEAP, 2008, p4). However, as there are so many different aspects to the skills of referencing and using sources, it is likely that your teachers, especially those new to your course, will need to check and clarify some individual examples once they start marking. Doing so should help your team to achieve a more standardised approach to identifying and marking plagiarism and poor academic practice, and therefore should be encouraged. When teachers are more experienced at marking, they may be able to discuss such problematic cases with their second marker. However, if significant plagiarism is detected, the student in question will need to have a formal meeting of some kind, as determined by your institution.

Below is the wording added to the end of our rubric. You can see highlighted the instruction on how to deal with plagiarism, but, as previously stated, teachers may need to check their interpretation of the extent of the plagiarism and the impact they have made on the student's mark with more experienced team members or managers.

> The mark is selected by looking at the assignment for **overall task fulfilment** (as indicated by the **strapline** in bold for each band) in order to determine which band it best fits. Once the band has been selected, the mark for the piece of work will move up or down **within the band** according to how well the assignment fulfils each of the descriptors in that band. If **plagiarism** is present, this will override the other descriptors in the band. The extent to which work is copied from sources will determine how much the mark is affected on a case-by-case basis. It is not only the content element that is affected; plagiarism can also impact the language element of the task significantly as it is not the student's own.

Through benchmarking

In order to become familiar with the level expected of the students in a particular assessment task, it is important for markers to see examples first. As is generally the case, it is useful to find more than one example so that the differences between levels can be examined. Benchmarking is one way of doing this.

What we mean here by 'benchmarking' is taking samples that have previously been marked and standardised by at least two experienced markers. You select these samples to show to your teachers, together with the feedback, comments, and marks awarded. One advantage of giving your teachers benchmarked samples is that it removes any potential discomfort of individuals having to give out their mark to the group. This is especially important when you have new members of staff joining your team as teachers have told us that they can experience feelings of being judged when asked to call out their marks in standardisation meetings. Individual teachers may worry that, if they are not in the same range as the rest of the group, their performance will be watched or monitored in some way or that they are inadequate for the task. Any such negative feelings amongst your team may also subsequently negatively impact their confidence and/or performance as a marker or even as a teacher in extreme cases. Therefore, using benchmarked samples avoids all of this by allowing markers to see the comments and marks, and then aligning themselves to the standards these benchmarks set.

Standardisation

More experienced staff may not need benchmarked samples, so, if you have a 'mature' teaching team, you may wish to jump straight to standardisation. This is where you give out unmarked samples to your marking team and ask each one to complete the marking individually and come to the meeting ready to share their marks with the rest of the team. They will also need to be able to justify why they have awarded the marks they have given. As we have said, this type of marking can cause stress even for experienced markers, so you might want to consider whether to still use benchmarking as a first step to standardisation. However, standardisation meetings of this kind are an important tool to consider. Discussions between all team members can be very productive in leading towards a shared understanding of the principles and philosophy of the course even if there is some pain and loss of face involved. The key here is to keep this to an absolute minimum. Maybe putting teachers in pairs to discuss their individual marks before talking to the whole team could help with this. Or perhaps using an anonymous approach with a Microsoft Forms document or other equivalent. To be avoided at all costs is the standardisation meeting where the 'boss' goes round the room individually asking each teacher for their mark and then writing it down. It may be done in all innocence, but such actions by those in positions of power and authority can breed paranoia.

Second or double marking

For the purposes of this guide, we will not differentiate between second or double marking.

Although, technically, it could be argued that second marking is done at a later date than the first making, whilst double marking is done simultaneously.

What we mean here by second or double marking is a quality control check on the first marking, however this is done. There are a number of ways in which this can be approached, and these might be different for oral and written work, and the percentage of second marking may differ too. Sometimes all assessments are second marked, whereas it is also possible that there is a specific number or percentage required. This varies between institutions, so you will need to check yours to make sure that you are doing the right thing.

You will need to keep a record of this for quality control purposes as you will most likely be asked about this.

Below is an example of a moderation form:

School of Languages, Cultures, and Societies
Moderation Form

Module:	Date:
First Marker:	Moderator:

Please specify any particular scripts that you would like the moderator to look at:
Additional comments for the moderator:
Scripts/marks to moderator (date):

Proportion of scripts moderated (number or percentage):
Moderator's comments:
Suggested action:
Action taken:

Notes: Moderators should moderate **25%** of scripts **OR** at least **ten** scripts (whichever is the greater number of scripts of the *whole module cohort*).

Moderators should **indicate** on exam scripts/evaluation feedback form that they have been moderated (countersign).

Blind marking

This means that the second marker marks in exactly the same way as the first marker; without any access to the mark awarded or feedback given. The first and second markers then come together and compare marks and notes in order to arrive at a final mark.

The issues with this approach are that it is perhaps more time consuming and without any real benefit. Whereas, if the second marker marks with access to the mark awarded by the first marker, they are looking to see if they agree with that and the feedback given.

With blind second marking, there is more room for conflict and ultimately for the one who shouts the loudest to get their own way. Marking with full access to feedback and comments should reduce this possibility.

Alongside this, as we have said previously, it is important for the team leader or manager to make appropriate pairings between staff.

Oral assessment marking

Because of the dynamic nature of oral assessment, whether they are group tasks or individual ones, we believe that they should be double marked. This, however, we are aware may be difficult in the case of the lone EAP teacher in a centre. It may be that there are subject teachers who can lend a hand, though, so do reach out to them and ask for their help. Whether you do this by one person focusing more on content and one more on language and delivery, or by both assessing all elements of the oral task, will depend on the individual pairings. It might be more practical to take the former approach where the second marker is a subject specialist, but it can be an equally valid approach for two EAP teachers to take also. However you decide to work, it will need to be agreed between the two of you.

Sometimes second marking is undertaken by means of a video recording of the assessments. We don't recommend this as a first choice for second marking since there are a number of things missing in a recording that are present in live performances. For example, the atmosphere is not adequately captured on film and there may be body language or gestures between people that are not captured on the recording. The quality of recordings can also vary and it may be difficult to hear some parts of a student's turn. They may speak too quietly for the microphone to pick up what they are saying or there may be background noise interfering with audibility. Builders, sirens, livestock, etc., can all have their impact on the day. All of these factors can therefore impact the mark awarded and we have found that the second mark can be up to a band lower from that of the live assessment. Therefore, for greater consistency and standardisation, we suggest that recordings should only be used as a last resort in an emergency situation. For example, one of the two assessors is taken ill and can't attend, no stand-in can be found at short notice and the only option is to proceed with a single assessor. In such cases, the second marking will have to be undertaken at a later date by means of recordings. If you find yourself in a position where you are single marking using the full rubric, this might be too much to handle. In fact, you might feel like that whether or not you are single marking. If you have unwieldy rubric, you may wish to use a simplified grid such as the one below.

Presentation marking grid

Name of student: **Date:**

	80+	79–70	69–65	64–60	59–55 Standard expected level	54–50	49–45	44–40	39–30	29–20
Content and organisation										
Response to questions										
Use of sources										
Fluency and Cohesion										
Grammar and Lexis										
Pronunciation										
Visual Communication										

Assessor 1: Assessor 2:

Mark for content: Mark for content:

Mark for Language: Mark for Language:

External Examiners

In any case, you will need to record your oral assessments so that the External Examiner can view a random sample when they come to moderate your course. All trustworthy IFY courses need to be externally moderated in order to maintain standards in the sector as a whole. In some cases, this may be done centrally, where all the relevant materials are sent from the centre to a Head Office, so you may never meet your External Examiner face to face. In such cases, feedback may be given remotely or you may receive written feedback only.

However, regardless of whether the External Examiner's visit is face to face or remote, it should be viewed as an opportunity not a threat. If you are running an IFY course, especially if this is for the first time, they will be able to give you valuable feedback on your strengths and weaknesses. They will have an overview of other provision with which to make comparisons and they may be able to make some suggestions that you would not have thought of by yourself. (Once you have gained more experience of IFY, becoming an External Examiner yourself is a great way of getting access to other people's courses and to see all the different ways in which things can be done.) Use the moderation process as an opportunity to have discussions about your practice. Often, especially for the lone teacher, there isn't much chance to do this and it can be an enjoyable and rewarding experience. If, as we have said, your examiner is not physically present at your centre, this 'discussion' may take the form of a written report in which you address particular things you wish the examiner to know or advise you about.

The External Examiner will also write a report after their visit as part of the moderation process. These reports are read by people in higher positions within your institution or organisation who may be able to change something. So, if there is anything that isn't working in your institution and that isn't being acted upon, it may be that, through your communication with the External Examiner, these issues can be highlighted in their report and picked up on by someone reading it. In this way, you may find that issues are then resolved.

Before the External Examiner's visit, they will most likely require access to course documentation. This is so that they can familiarise themselves with the course specifications. Any documents that give this overview, such as course handbooks for example, should be sent to them in advance of their visit so that the time they are with you can be spent in talking to the manager(s) and teaching team, possibly also to a small group of students, sampling work, and confirming marks/grades. This may involve attending a progression meeting, as it would at our institution. In order to do their job, they need access to all course-related documentation. In particular, they need to see each assessment task, marking rubric, evidence of internal moderation of marks, mark sheets alongside samples of student work for each assessment (probably a range of different bands and/or different markers). They may also wish to see course teaching materials and worksheets, so you need to be well-prepared both beforehand and on the day, to make sure there is organisation and easy access to everything related to your course. All files and documents should be present and complete, all marks entered in the relevant place(s) and everything should be transparent and clear to outside eyes and ears.

The impacts of Covid-19

As with everything else connected to learning, teaching, and assessment during the pandemic, most, if not all, activities were carried out remotely. The first year this happened, we didn't build in time for our External Examiners to 'meet' and chat with module leads. This resulted in a few misunderstandings about specific features of some of our provision that could have been avoided. We learned from that, so the second year we built in this time for meetings before moderation began and every External Examiner commented in the board meetings how useful this part of the process had been. At the time of writing, the extent to which changes from physical visits to remote ones will remain in place is unclear, but it is likely that there will be some lasting impacts that change practices forever.

Reflective team task

Now you are at the end of this chapter, here are some questions for you and your team to discuss together.

> These discussions may help your team to bond, discover any potential pitfalls before they arise, and generally get to know one another better before you start teaching and assessing together.
>
> - What makes a 'good' manager?
> - What makes a 'good' team member?
> - What are your most positive memories of being managed? Why is this?
> - How do you react to criticism? Why is this?
> - Is your answer different if it's professional or personal criticism? Why is this?
> - What is your most memorable instance of conflict? Why is this?
> - How could this conflict have been de-escalated? Successfully resolved?
> - How organised are you?
> - What, if anything, are you going to find most challenging about teaching and assessing on this module?
> - What, if anything, are you most looking forward to about teaching and assessing on this module?
>
> These questions focus on attitudes to assessment and might help you standardise your approach as a team:
>
> - To what extent should you penalise for plagiarism, cheating, or malpractice?
> - To what extent should you penalise for non-task fulfilment?
> - How much of a script should you annotate for language errors?
> - Which area(s) of the rubric and/or the task should you give feedback on?

- How important do you think it is to use specific descriptors from the marking rubric in your feedback?
- Are any of your answers different for formative vs summative work? Why is this?

References

BALEAP. 2008. *Competency Framework for Teachers of English for Academic Purposes.* [Online]. [Accessed 16 January 2019]. Available from: www.baleap.org/wp-content/uploads/2016/04/teap-competency-framework.pdf

Charles, M. and Pecorari, D. 2016. *Introducing English for Academic Purposes.* Oxon and New York: Routledge.

Cottrell, S. 2001. *Teaching Study Skills and Supporting Learning.* Basingstoke: Palgrave.

Council of Europe. 2021. Common European Framework of Reference for Languages: Learning, Teaching, Assessment (CEFR). [Online]. [Accessed 12 July 2020]. Available from: www.coe.int/en/web/common-european-framework-reference-languages/home

Davies, A. 1990. *Principles of Language Testing.* Massachusetts, USA: Blackwell.

de Chazal, E. 2014. *English for Academic Purposes.* China: Oxford University Press.

Handley, F. J. L. and Read, A. 2016. Developing assessment policy and evaluating practice: a case study of the introduction of a new marking scheme. *Perspectives: Policy and Practice in Higher Education.* **21** (4), pp135–139.

Hübner, A. 2000. Assessment and accreditation of languages: implications for tutor training. In Hübner, A., Ibarz, T., and Laviosa. eds. *Assessment and Accreditation for Languages: The Emerging Consensus?* London: C*i*LT, pp81–102.

Keating, K. 2019. 11 things we know about marking and two things we don't … yet. 5 March. *The Ofqual blog.* [Accessed 3 September 2019]. Available from: https://ofqual.blog.gov.uk/2019/03/05/14572/

Manning, A. 2016. *Assessing EAP Theory and Practice in Assessment Literacy.* Reading: Garnet.

Newton, F. J, Wright, J. D., and Newton, J. D. 2014. Skills training to avoid inadvertent plagiarism: results from a randomised study. *Higher Education Research and Development.* **33** (6), pp1180–1193.

Rhead, S and Black, B. 2018. *Marking Consistency Metrics.* [Online]. [Accessed 3 September 2019]. Coventry: Ofqual. Available from: https://assets.publishing.service.gov.uk/government/uploads/system/uploads/attachment_data/file/759207/Marking_consistency_metrics_-_an_update_-_FINAL64492.pdf

Schmitt, D and Hamp-Lyons, L. 2015. The need for EAP teacher knowledge in Assessment. *Journal of English for Academic Purposes.* **18**, pp3–8.

6 Personal tutoring

Relevant BALEAP competency:

Student Needs:
5. *An EAP teacher will understand the requirements of the target context that students wish to enter as well as the needs of students in relation to their prior learning experiences and how these might influence their current educational expectations.*

(BALEAP, 2008)

Before beginning this section, it is worth considering the role of academic teaching staff in UK HE institutions regarding the relationships we have with our students. As teaching staff, we tend to have dual, and sometimes conflicting, roles as academic tutor *and* personal tutor. This can place us in a precarious position, on the one hand being sympathetic to a student's personal difficulties as personal tutor, then on the other being responsible for giving the student a mark they may not be happy with as academic tutor. This can lead to tutors having anxieties around personal tutoring if they also happen to also be a student's academic tutor. This particular dual role may not be the case in your institution, but nevertheless the role of personal tutor alone is a demanding, challenging, and time-consuming role, and requires a whole set of skills that we're often (as language/skills tutors) not naturally equipped with.

The UK Advisory and Tutoring Association (UKAT) (2019) have a comprehensive list of the competencies required by personal tutors on their website: *conceptual, informational, relational,* and *professional,* plus the sub-skills that make up each of these competencies, which are essentially the expectations your student and your institution will have of you in your personal tutoring role. Although UKAT is a useful resource for those involved in personal tutoring, reading through the competencies can induce anxiety, particularly when you remember this is just one aspect of your job as a foundation year tutor. Tutors with some experience tend to be acutely aware of what students need in terms of their personal welfare and support, but trying to balance that with other demands on time can be stressful. It may be a part of our job we find fulfilling and interesting as it is an opportunity to play an active role in a student's development and this can be very rewarding, however, institutions do not always fully understand the impact the personal tutoring role can have on a tutor's workload. This is not only in terms of the hours it takes to do the job well, but the emotional toll. This has never been truer than during the past two years as Covid-19 and its impacts on the student community have made the job more challenging and, if you are a dedicated and caring personal tutor, this will most likely have taken its toll on you, too.

Luck, in her 2010 article, highlights very clearly the boundary issues for tutors as they try to negotiate their roles, and ten years later discussions around this still feature large in informal staff discussions. She also mentions the fact that education is 'emotional' and this is what makes teaching and tutoring a challenge, an aspect of our profession that I don't think we often acknowledge; students invest a lot of their lives (and finances) in getting a university education and success or otherwise is very much bound up with feelings of self-worth. Even the most experienced tutors still worry about 'how do I tell **student A** that they very likely won't make the grade in my module?' The chapter on assessment deals with this issue under 'managing student expectations' and 'blame culture', but personal tutorials are usually the arenas where these frustrations are played out and having some insight into how to handle the many possible scenarios is the best way to support your students and to feel more confident in your role.

Background

One of the responsibilities of IFY tutors might be that of **academic personal tutor** (APT) to a group of students. As IFY students tend to be relatively young (some under 18), and many living and studying in a foreign country, or away from the family home, for the first time, they need strong and consistent support during this important transition in their lives, and indeed *'social and emotional well-being'* is identified by Advance HE (2014) as one of the main issues of concern for international students. Therefore, one of the key roles of an APT should be to encourage students to contact them regarding any issues they may have, academic or personal, and to help students understand the value of timely communication, so that they are not prevented from reaching their potential.

Different institutions may vary, but, usually, as an APT you will be required to see your tutee group individually at least three times over the course of the year and to be available for one 'office hour' every week so that your tutees can drop in, if necessary, without an appointment. At a very basic level, you will be required to make a written record of what was discussed during these sessions and to pass on any necessary information as appropriate to the relevant people, or to find out anything the student might have questions about that you do not know the answer to and report back to them. By 'relevant people', this may mean other tutors who have contact with the student or someone in the admin team (with the student's permission if the situation requires this). These written records can be accessed by students if they request it, so tutors should always write them with this in mind. At Leeds, we use a specific online system to store all the details of tutorials, which is used throughout the student's academic life at the university, but any secure online space would be appropriate.

The discussions between the APT and the tutee are confidential; however, it is essential that any information that concerns a student's physical or mental welfare be shared with another member of staff – usually someone who is in a senior position, for example, the director of the overall programme. Appropriate action will then be taken depending on the severity of the situation. For example, students could be referred to the Student Counselling Service if they needed to talk to a professional or the GP if they were physically unwell. However, if the situation is more serious and a student is threatening self-harm or harm to others, this should be quickly escalated and each university will have its own policy for dealing with this rapidly and safely. It is important that APTs do not keep any information of a serious nature to themselves as it can be extremely stressful, and potentially life-threatening for the student, and this must also be made clear to students at the outset of personal tutoring.

Under 18s

HE establishments have an enhanced duty of care towards under 18s and that is because, under English law, anyone under the age of 18 is regarded as a child according to the 1989 Children Act (Guidance on the admission of young persons and children and on safeguarding students under 18 and adult students in vulnerable circumstances) (University of Leeds, 2016). While it is the responsibility of the institution to allow under 18s admission to a programme of study, at the same time they must ensure that they are providing a 'reasonably safe environment'; so, this will involve a risk assessment by the institution. Every institution will have similar guidance in place and, indeed, foundation year programmes may have their own more tailored documentation to disseminate to all staff who come into contact with under 18s. It is the job of module leaders to ensure that all teaching staff understand how this impacts on them in a practical sense in the contact they have with students as class tutors and/or APTs.

As a large minority of foundation year students are under 18, safeguarding needs to be considered carefully in discussions around personal tutoring, but it also has implications for other areas of academic life, for example, any planned trips off campus where risk assessments are needed under a university's Risk Management of Events Protocol. Under-18s should always be immediately identified to staff so that they are able to plan for any possible risks both on and off campus and to ensure that there is a correct staff to student ratio.

Class tutors, APTs, and indeed anyone who comes into contact with under 18s must be checked by the Disclosure and Barring Service (DBS) on a regular basis. This is one of the ways to mitigate any risks, but there are many others. The University of Leeds *Guidance on the admission of young persons and children and on safeguarding students under 18 and adults in vulnerable circumstances,* appendix 5 paragraph 2, (2016, referred to in the university's policy on safeguarding children, young persons and adults in vulnerable circumstances, 2016) states that: '*staff should take steps to ensure that they do not put themselves in a position where an allegation of abuse can be made against them*'. Therefore, in order to safeguard both students *and* APTs, every activity and action needs to be thought through carefully, bearing any guidelines in mind. For example, it is advisable that tutorials should take place somewhere that is reasonably public – in a common room, for example, or in a room where you are visible (either glass walls/doors or the door open), but where the tutor feels that there is enough privacy so that students do not feel uncomfortable discussing personal issues. Similarly, if you ever need to talk to an under-18 student about anything after a class, it is always a good idea to have a colleague present in the room or to move to a more 'public' space. The Leeds guidelines also state very clearly that tutors should only contact a student within their university role and not via phone, text or social media. If you have a Facebook account, for example, a student may seek you out with the best friendly intentions and make a friend request; in these circumstances, it is best to decline the request and then explain to the student why. The general rule of thumb is to keep your work life and personal life separate and, no matter how much you care about your students, they fall into the former category.

All the above should be highlighted by module leaders in staff induction so that everyone is following the correct procedure and staff should be told that, if in doubt, they should always double-check with the module or programme leader. The safeguarding of children is always rather a 'grey area' at HE institutes (HEIs) because there is no specific statutory duty for HEIs to do this as there is in schools, for example, which can lead to a lack of consistency across the sector (guidance on the admission of young persons and children and on safeguarding students under 18 and adult students in vulnerable circumstances) (University of Leeds, 2016). However, institutions should be ensuring that they provide as safe an environment as they can and always err on the side of caution. The British Council (2014), experienced as it is in providing summer schools and courses for young children, has some very comprehensive guidance in its *Care of Under 18s: Guidance for ELT Providers* report (see reference list for further details).

Confidentiality

'Confidentiality' is a crucial part of personal tutoring and it is necessary to bear in mind the following:

> *Within the institution*: Only pass on information when there is good reason to do so, that is, when you think the student may be in danger or may put others in danger. If you are worried about a student's welfare then do not keep this to yourself, but the key is to *'be discrete'* and not to discuss students' personal problems in the staffroom over lunch or on the train journey home.
>
> *Outside the institution:* You can only communicate information about the student to their friends and family when you have been given written permission to do so by the student.
>
> If it is a parent who is worried about not having had contact with their child or asks about academic progress, then all you can do is pass on the message and encourage the student to make contact, or alternatively contact the student and ask for them to send you their written permission by email. Even students who are under 18 have a right to privacy in this respect and we should not disclose anything to parents unless we have the child's permission to do so (University of Leeds, 2016).

The only time confidentiality can be broken is if there is a risk that the student may harm themselves, or when the law requires it.

> *Keeping records*: Make sure that the information in records is clear, concise, and, as mentioned earlier, non-judgemental, as students do have the right to see any of the files held on them. We tend to write down the outcome of each tutorial not in the third person as some APTs prefer, but as if we are talking to the student. Any very sensitive information that the student has told you should be written in a way that shows you have taken note of the issue but doesn't necessarily outline all the details. For example, if a student is upset about a relationship break-up, you may want to write *'we discussed the particular issue that has been upsetting you and you have decided to seek help from student counselling with this'*. During the first tutorial, it is always a good idea to explain to the students that you will be writing up notes in this way and that it will be confidential.

Practical help for students: Pastoral

As a personal tutor, you are not expected to be able to 'fix' all student problems or to be an expert counsellor, and this is particularly true in cases of mental health and well-being. Some tutors are naturals at dealing with pastoral issues and are able to assuage student worries and strike the correct balance between sympathy and professionalism, others may feel uncomfortable with the 'counsellor' role but are effective and efficient at directing students to the right kind of help; what needs to be stressed here is that not everyone can be the 'textbook' personal tutor.

It is always a good idea to begin the first tutorial by emphasising that there are limits to the support you can provide and that you are not a trained counsellor, but you can listen and refer the student to someone who is, if that is necessary. It is important that you try to keep a professional distance from students as much as is possible to avoid placing yourself in a difficult situation. It sometimes takes an enormous amount of willpower to not express your true feelings regarding a student's situation, particularly when you are very much on the student's side and feel they have been wronged. Luck (2010) refers to an exaggerated version of this as 'omnipotence', whereby an inexperienced APT may respond to a student's gratitude at their help by feeling that they are the only one who can support this student and protect them from an uncaring and bureaucratic institution. This can end up with the tutor becoming too emotionally involved, thus causing real damage to the relationship and failing the student in the end. There is also this cautionary note from Hughes et al. (p57, 2018 cited in Lochtie et al., 2018) *'legal advice suggests that if you provide ongoing support and this goes wrong you will be judged not against the qualities of a well-meaning academic but as that of a trained and experienced counsellor'*. Students are often just wanting to share a problem with you, but, if this is not enough and you feel out of your depth, use the network of university professional services. If, for example, a student is having difficulty sleeping, you may need to direct them to see their GP in the first instance, or if the student has had a bereavement then a referral to student counselling may be the best option, plus advice on mitigating circumstances if this has affected their studies.

Most HE institutions have online information for students, which includes lists of email addresses and phone numbers for these services, but APTs are advised to have a copy of this to hand, too. Students may not always pay these services much attention (at universities during Freshers' Week they are always visible), until they really need them, or may not even know of their existence. Similarly, some cultures do not always appreciate them as sharing your intimate problems with strangers may not be acceptable or may feel uncomfortable, however, others are willing to try, and can find them supportive and beneficial. *Confidentiality is key* and it must always be stressed to students that private problems are confidential unless circumstances are deemed to be dangerous or life-threatening.

Any underlying medical issues should have been flagged up by the student when applying to the programme and will have been passed on to you as APT, but it is always a good idea to ask the student to let you know of any special requirements they may have that might affect their work in the classroom or performance in examinations. For the latter, you may need to direct the student to disability services so that special arrangements can be made for exams, such as time extensions.

Special circumstances

If a student is experiencing an overwhelming personal issue, which is preventing them from focusing on their studies, this is the opportunity for the personal tutor to explain the processes the institution has in place for these situations. For example, arrangements may need to be made for an extension to any assessments or the student may have to apply for mitigating circumstances. In both cases, the student will need to evidence the claim for mitigation/extension and attach these to the application. All the documentation regarding extensions, mitigating circumstances, and policies surrounding these, should be digitally stored where both students and tutors can access them easily.

One final, but critical point, is that, as an APT who also teaches their tutees, you may only ever see your students in a classroom setting, which is quite a 'guided' scenario and one where, superficially, students may all appear to be getting along famously. Sometimes it may be easy to spot the student who does not seem to be making friends with the others or who appears awkward or is left out of group discussions. At the tutorial, this may prompt the question 'have you made friends/connections with other students?' or 'are you finding time to socialise with others?' The student's world *outside the classroom* is one we don't see as tutors, it is complex and bound by all kinds of cultural rules we may not necessarily be aware of, and this may be where issues lie. As we are dealing with international students, there may be clashes between their own culture and the new one they are experiencing. An example of this was a female student who was being talked about and ostracised by some of the other female students in the same nationality group in the year because it was felt she was being 'too friendly' with one of the boys (they had been studying together a lot). This situation was making her feel uncomfortable. It was never evident from the way she behaved in class that anything was amiss and the only way I knew about this was when she made an appointment to see me. She was an open and confident person by nature and so contacting me as her APT to talk about a very personal issue was the obvious step for her. However, not all students feel able to make that step and ask for an impromptu meeting with a tutor, therefore it is particularly important to ask the right questions during arranged tutorials so students are given an opportunity to divulge anything that is bothering them. In this situation, I was not able to do much; the student didn't feel she was being bullied, although we discussed this and the steps I could take on her behalf. She simply wanted to offload and, after checking in on her every so often, she said that the problem had eventually faded away. The moral of this tale is that students have lives outside the classroom and, just because they are achieving the grades, it does not necessarily mean that all is well.

Practical help for students: Academic

On the Leeds IFY programme, the APT is also the semester 1 class tutor and is therefore aware of how a student is developing academically in their particular module at least. According to Leeds University guidelines, APTs should *'foster a supportive and effective academic partnership'* with their tutees, but what does this mean in reality? Most foundation year programmes involve students studying several subjects across the institution and so one of the responsibilities of the personal tutor is to ask students how they are faring in each of these subjects. It may be relatively easy to help a student with academic issues in your own subject area as you may have seen the problem at first hand and will no doubt have resources to hand to guide the student and monitor progress. With other subjects, for instance, if a student is struggling with maths, it is a good idea to ask the students what they are currently doing to deal with the problem, for example, have they spoken to the tutor in question? Have they spoken to their peers (if it's something they didn't understand in a lecture)? If the issue is more to do with the delivery of a lecture – have they spoken with the student representative who will raise it at the staff-student forum? If the issue lies with another module and the complaint is about another tutor, then a certain amount of sensitivity and diplomacy is required. It is never a good idea for a personal tutor to directly email the tutor in question or to appear confrontational in any way, but rather the student should be encouraged to engage with the tutor in question or, if there are a number of students with a similar issue, then to raise it with the student rep, who will in turn raise it at a staff-student forum if this exists in your institution.

Not all students will have a mature and responsible attitude towards studying and tutorials may be the time to discuss things such as lateness to class if this has been an issue, or attitude towards studying, or even participation in class activities. Sensitivity is always required as the underlying causes of any of these issues cannot be guessed at. For example, for the first few days of studying in the UK, some students may be late simply because they have not yet adjusted to UK time.

Tutorials are the time to flag up any issues with academic progress. At Leeds, the most crucial time for IFY students is February, when they will have completed semester 1 assessments and exams and will have the results of these. Whichever institution you are working in, there will be a time of year when you will need to take stock of a student's progress and their ability to enter their degree programme of choice. This is the point when a tutor may need to have some 'difficult' conversations with students who are not making the grade and encourage them to have a 'plan B' regarding undergraduate study. It may be a good idea to have a box of tissues to hand at these tutorials. Honesty is always the best policy and the more experience you have working on foundation year programmes, the better you will be able to judge a student's abilities and suggest alternatives. Tutors need to be fully aware of the specific entry requirements for the variety of degree programmes tutees are moving onto and discussions on how to approach students who are currently 'failing' should be had at staff meetings.

The personal tutor: Friend or mentor?

This strongly ties in with your personality as a tutor, but, generally speaking, it is better to keep the relationship on a professional footing and to avoid getting too personally involved with students and their problems. This is often easier said than done as foundation year students are young and far from home, making them vulnerable, plus you may have built up a very good relationship with them during class time. However, your well-being as a tutor is at stake if you become too involved in a student's personal life. Luck (2010) cites cases of tutors who have given students their personal details and lived to regret it. There must be boundaries for everyone's well-being and it is never a good idea to give students your personal phone number or to invite them to your home, however lonely, homesick, or stressed a student may appear to be. Never put yourself at risk in this way. It is important that staff maintain clear boundaries between professional and personal life and, again, there are other support systems in the university that are there to take over when you as a personal tutor cannot help. Both tutor and student need to be aware of these boundaries and they should be outlined from the first session. International students, especially, may not understand what you are or aren't responsible for and may be demanding and want to contact you about everything when first arriving in the UK for study simply because the concept of a 'personal tutor' is unknown to them and the word 'personal' could be construed to mean 'a service that is available whenever I need it'.

If a student is referred to another agency in the university, then you need to follow up with this so that the tutee feels they have not just been passed onto someone else. You need to know what these support systems are and what they provide, from the location of the Islamic prayer room through to student counselling services.

If you have an office hour or 'drop-in' time, ensure that students know to email you and make an appointment outside of this time and that they cannot just expect a tutor to be free to talk to them if they turn up unexpectedly. It is important, though, for students to know that you *are* concerned about their personal welfare and that any missed classes or missed tutorials are a cause for concern and will be followed up.

Are there any personal tutoring issues that may be specific to IFY students?

Foundation year students may not be familiar with a number of aspects of culture in the general sense of being in the UK (although this may not be the case for all students) and in the academic sense. They may also be suffering from homesickness and an enormous feeling of culture shock. What we may perceive as rudeness or laziness may be the student behaving as they normally would at 'home' and, although an induction week[1] tries to make students aware of cultural differences and what is deemed 'acceptable behaviour' in the UK, the tutorial is often the time when these things can be discussed sensitively. Students may be foxed by change in routine (three-hour classes are a particular issue), language, food, weather, just having to take care of themselves (cooking for themselves, doing the laundry) is often a huge challenge in itself! Luck (2010) mentions that students may expect to replicate the relationship they had with their high-school teacher, and the tutor may need to explain sensitively, perhaps in the induction sessions, how those relationships differ. Some students have come from small high schools with very strong teacher-pupil bonds, and they have to understand that this cannot be replicated at university. Tutors also have to learn to be sensitive to, and tolerant of, a student's religious, personal, and cultural needs even if they contradict what the tutor believes.

Reflective team task

Now you are at the end of this chapter, here are some questions and case studies for you and your team to discuss together:

- What have you found most challenging about being an APT?
- Does your institution have clear guidelines surrounding the safeguarding of under 18s? Do you feel confident in dealing with this age group as an APT?
- Do you feel there is enough support available for APTs at your institution? If not, what kind of support would you like?
- How effective do you feel you are as an APT on a scale of 1–10, one being ineffective and ten being extremely effective? How can you justify this?
- Discuss how, as an APT, you might deal with the following scenarios:
    1. **Student A** explains that they have an issue with a tutor from one of the other IFY modules. This tutor does not explain things clearly in the lectures and this seems to be a feeling across the whole cohort according to student A. Student A is also not sure why they got such a low mark in a recent test in this module.
    2. **Student B** has an issue with two other students in their class. Student B explains that, when they are asked to work together, the two students either ignore student B's contributions or mock their accent. Student B is worried because the module tutor has put them all together for a group assessment on another module and is concerned that the grade will be impacted if they cannot work well together.

3   **Student C** is living in university accommodation and the student in the next room is very noisy, playing music until the early hours and having friends in the room for parties during the week. Student C is finding it hard to focus on studying and has difficulty sleeping with the noise, this means they feel tired and unable to concentrate in lectures. They have politely asked the neighbour to turn down the music, this happens for a while but then the volume creeps back up again. It has got to the point where Student C wants to give up studying and go back home.

(Answer key below.)

Answer key

Student A

The APT needs to find out what exactly the student means by the tutor 'not explaining clearly' to determine whether this is indeed a tutor rushing through material or if it is the student having difficulty with listening and understanding. If it is the former, then the student should be encouraged to contact the tutor in question and, if they do not feel comfortable about doing that, then it could be raised by the student rep at the staff/student forum, which most institutions have in place. If it is an issue with listening and understanding, the tutor may want to suggest some strategies to help with this.

As for the low mark in the test, the student should be encouraged to email the tutor, or talk to the tutor after class to ask for feedback. Tell the student you will follow up with them on this. Students often feel uncomfortable about approaching lecturers in this way, but it is a skill they need to have. You might want to briefly run through what they might say to the tutor to build confidence!

Student B

Sympathy needed here for student B. It sounds like low-level bullying and HE institutions do not tolerate this and will have a robust policy for staff and students to follow on *dignity and mutual respect*. Students should be made aware of this policy in induction week, but of course this is not always enough to deter these behaviours.

It is hard to solve this issue without breaking confidentiality as the accused will need to know who is accusing them so that they can explain the situation from their perspective, but confidentiality should be maintained as far as it is possible to do so. Student B as the 'victim' may not want to pursue this further for fear of reprisals, so this needs to be handled very sensitively indeed. However, this should not act as

> a barrier to thoroughly investigating this complaint. It will be necessary to inform a senior member of staff, perhaps the head of the IFY programme, and they may wish to take it forward. Try not to immediately think badly of those being accused, there could be all kinds of reasons for this situation arising and they could be borne out of simple misunderstandings due to students' different cultures.
>
> Depending on the outcome of this investigation, it may be necessary to contact Student B's tutor in the module where the group assessment is taking place and ask her to change the groupings in as discrete a way as possible if this is necessary.
>
> *Student C*
>
> I think the next step for this student would be to approach the accommodation warden whose responsibility it is to deal with these issues. In an HE setting, these tend to be post-grad students who have a little more gravitas when dealing with undergrads not following accommodation rules and regs. If this does not have the desired results, then as APT I would email the warden myself and explain what is happening, outlining the impact on the student's well-being and ability to study. Until the issue is fully resolved, you could suggest that the student use the library or computer cluster to study or, if possible, stay with a friend if they are desperate for a good night's sleep. Always remember to keep checking in with the student so that they don't think you've forgotten about them and also to ensure that the situation has been fully resolved.

Note

1 We are aware that not all institutions offer an induction week and that this tends to be mostly universities or institutions that have the capacity (of time and staff) to do so. However, it might be a good idea to at least offer some distance induction, this may be a recorded session with some input from students, such as completing online questionnaires, the results of which could be used in the first teaching session(s).

References

Advance HE. 2014. *Life Outside the Classroom.* [Online]. [Accessed 7 February 2020]. Available from: www.advance-he.ac.uk/knowledge-hub/life-outside-classroom

BALEAP. 2008. *Competency Framework for Teachers of English for Academic Purposes.* [Online]. [Accessed 16 January 2019]. Available from: www.baleap.org/wp-content/uploads/2016/04/teap-competency-framework.pdf

Lochtie, D., McIntosh, E., Stork, A., and Walker, B. W. 2018. *Effective Personal Tutoring in Higher Education.* St Albans: Critical Publishing.

Luck, C. 2010. Challenges faced by tutors in higher education. *Psychodynamic Practice. Individuals, Groups and Organisations.* **16** (3), pp273–287.

The British Council. 2014. *Care of Under 18s: Guidance for ELT Providers.* [Online]. [Accessed 21 July 2021]. Available from: Criteria relating to students under-18 (www.britishcouncil.org)

The University of Leeds. 2016. *Guidance on the admission of young persons and children and on safeguarding students under 18 and adult students in vulnerable circumstances* referred to in *University Policy on safeguarding children, young persons and adults in vulnerable circumstances.* [Online]. [Accessed 12 July 2021]. Available from safeguarding_policy.pdf (www.leeds.ac.uk)

UK Advising and Tutoring. 2019. The UKAT Professional Framework for Advising and Tutoring. [Online]. [Accessed 11 January 2021]. Available from: www.ukat.ac.uk/standards/professional-framework-for-advising-and-tutoring/

7 Student autonomy and its place on IFY

Relevant BALEAP competency:

Student Autonomy:
7. *An EAP tutor will understand: the importance of student autonomy in academic contexts and will employ tasks, processes and interactions that require students to work effectively in groups or independently as appropriate.*

(BALEAP, 2008)

Student autonomy is now very much part and parcel of the learning experience for students in HE and we would be doing foundation year students a great disservice by not supporting them to become independent learners. The learning process does not end once foundation year is over and students will need to continue developing their academic skills and language; therefore, being able to manage their own learning is paramount.

At Leeds, part of the 'philosophy' of the IFY study skills module and part of our expectations as tutors is that students become far less dependent on the tutor than they might have been previously at high school. We define autonomy not only in the sense that students are able to understand their own strengths and weaknesses and set goals for themselves when it comes to their *learning*, but also in the broader sense of taking the initiative in all aspects of their student life, such as planning and thinking ahead, being proactive, asking when something is not clear, and being able to explain to, and negotiate with, tutors when necessary. The age of the typical IFY student is a significant determinant in the autonomy discussion and, because of their relative immaturity and the fact that they have just finished high school, they often rely very heavily on a tutor's input and support in reminding them of important dates and events and guiding them through study. On arrival at an HE institution anywhere in the world, students may struggle or even resist having to think for themselves above and beyond the basics that are required of them each day, particularly those who have a heavy academic timetable. There are other things in their lives outside of academia that they may need

DOI: 10.4324/9781003253624-7

to deal with for the first time, such as opening a bank account, dealing with landlords, cooking, and other domestic chores – often getting a quick answer from a tutor about anything related to study seems quicker than having to find out for themselves when their heads are full. In our experience, the first semester can be quite an overwhelming time for some students, particularly coming to terms with a new educational and living environment, and being unable to manage everything they are asked to do. There may be additional external pressures from parents and/or sponsors to succeed and we have had cases of students whose parents have been responsible for their choice of career path, leaving them wholly unmotivated and unwilling to engage with foundation year beyond a very superficial level.

This section of the book will explore ways of supporting students in becoming more autonomous: first in terms of their learning and second in terms of the other equally important aspects of their lives, thus avoiding overwhelming stress and anxiety. It also showcases reflective writing as a way of dealing with the former.

What do we mean by 'autonomy' at level zero?

'The concept of autonomy is grounded in a natural tendency for learners to take control over their learning ... Learners who lack autonomy are capable of developing it given appropriate conditions and preparation' (Benson, 2011). With this positive definition in mind, teaching materials should be designed knowing that all students have the capability to reach some degree of autonomy, but some may need more scaffolding than others. A further notion that should underpin the development of study skills programmes is Nunan's (2013) idea that autonomy is not an 'absolute concept' and exists at many levels, implying that autonomy does not necessarily mean working in isolation. We would not expect a foundation year student to work completely independently of the tutor and this should be made clear to both students and tutors. It may be more appropriate to use the term '*inter*dependence' for our students (Boud, 1981; Brookfield, 1986 cited in Palfreyman, 2005) with the emphasis on teamwork, that is, both tutor and student working together and collaborating on gaining the best results for the student. This may also help deal with the issue of 'blame culture' (see Chapter 4 for further discussion on this), as students see themselves as sharing responsibility for their learning and, ultimately, their grades. Most universities and FE institutions are now investing in the idea of 'partnership', that is, a process that brings students and staff together to make the educational experience more effective and inclusive for the student and tutor as stakeholders; therefore the 'teamwork' aspect of autonomy feeds into this ethos.

Nunan outlines various factors to be considered when a learner is trying to achieve autonomy, such as the personality of the learner, goals, the way in which the institution works, and the cultural context in which the learner is operating (Nunan, 1988 cited in Nunan, 2013). Culture will be examined separately below as this is often seen as being particularly relevant to this learner context considering the diversity of foundation year cohorts.

Cultural differences and their impact on autonomous learning

The cultural mix of foundation year programmes differs very much from institution to institution. At Leeds, the cohort tends to be mostly students from the Middle East (usually going on to study Medicine, Dentistry or STEM subjects) or from China (usually going on to study Business, Law and Design) with a sprinkling of other nationalities. The fact that most of the students on the programme are from China and the Middle East requires some discussion as autonomy in language learning has been very often linked to a student's culture, in the sense that it is a 'western' concept often found challenging for students from other cultures. A recent study by Alrabai (2017) on Saudi students' receptiveness to autonomous learning seems to support previous studies on this cohort in that it shows them to have low levels of responsibility and low involvement in self-direction activities, but with high ability and high motivation. However, the reasons Alrabai (2017) gives for these low levels are an education system that is very teacher-centred and heavily reliant on rote-learning. The study suggests that changes are needed in the Saudi education system to better prepare students for their future studies and to give them the tools they need to manage beyond the classroom. Some of the suggestions Alrabai makes are ones that we have already tried at Leeds and that have had positive results. Despite studies that tend to point to deficiencies in independent learning in non-western learners, at Leeds we tend to favour the view of Pennycook (2013) and Littlewood (1999), who, using East Asians as an example, have argued against the idea that non-western students cannot be autonomous. They believe that different aspects of autonomy need to be matched with the different needs of learners in different types of context, rather than relying on the idea of cultural interference. In fact, we tend to lean towards Nunan's earlier point and believe that, if the student is operating in a different cultural milieu, they are often more willing to accommodate new ideas than they might be at home in a familiar environment. Our classroom materials have been designed based on this idea, that there are no intrinsic differences that make East Asian or Middle Eastern learners any less capable of becoming autonomous learners than others. Alrabai (2017) mentions the following as effective ways of encouraging autonomy in his Saudi learners:

- learners becoming a source of information to other learners, such as information exchange activities and peer-correcting
- learners making decisions about the learning process
- learners evaluating or giving feedback on others' performance

- Task-based learning (TBL). This is mentioned as a way of supporting students to think differently about learning. We use this method at Leeds in our annotated bibliography assessment because of its learner-centredness and as an alternative to the usual PPP (Presentation-Practice-Production) method. It allows for learner experimentation and working independently of the tutor.

Motivation

Motivation and affective engagement are major players in the autonomy discussion, and this can often be at the root of any student's unwillingness to 'go the extra mile' with their learning. As a tutor, you hope that a student is invested in preparing for their future degree programme, but if that has been decided by someone else then that investment may well be non-existent. Parent, and even sponsor, expectations can place a huge burden on students in terms of trying to please when engagement is low. Anxiety and low esteem are also factors to consider. You may find there is the feeling from some students that coming from a state-run school as opposed to a private school (in their home country), for example, means that they are not as smart as their privately educated peers and will never achieve excellence. Discussions during personal tutorials can often uncover the reasons why a student is not engaged. Workload is another factor – students may be struggling to deal with the very basic study requirements and do not have the mental capacity for any extra work.

Alternatively, autonomous learning activities, because of their very individual and personal nature, can become a haven for some students and a place where, if handled sensitively by the tutor, can promote self-worth and real learning opportunities. This is often beneficial for more introverted students who may feel that, while they cannot always 'shine' in classroom discussions, for example, they can when working alone and that this is also seen by the tutor and valued. Students may also be experiencing issues with time management and autonomous activities can offer more flexibility by not being bound to class-time or strict deadlines.

Task-based learning (TBL) as a way of kick-starting autonomy in learners

The first assessment task that our students at Leeds are presented with in semester one is an annotated bibliography task. We feel this is a good initial task as it covers many of the micro-skills that are needed, and can be built upon as the year progresses, such as reading for specific information, choosing relevant information, paraphrasing, and summarising. The following is the task we have used with our healthcare cohort, and this is a practice task before they attempt the final task, which will be graded, and which will be on a different topic. For this practice task, we use the TBL methodology as we believe this is an opportunity to expose students to working without the heavy tutor input they may be used to at high school. This task is not too 'high risk' for students because it is a practice run of the real assessment task and so should not induce any feelings of panic.

Practice assessment task 1

To produce an annotated bibliography for an assignment topic

Imagine that you have been asked to write an essay with the following title:

> *Should patients be allowed lawful access to medical cannabis to treat the symptoms of chronic illnesses and/or the side effects of treatments? Discuss, providing evidence from sources to support your points.*

You must produce an annotated bibliography for the title above.

This task will assess your ability to:

- select appropriate information to answer an assignment question
- evaluate sources
- read and summarise academic sources (using appropriate reading, annotating, and note-making techniques)
- write an accurate list of references (using the Leeds Harvard referencing system), including a brief explanation of each source. Make sure this list *is in alphabetical order*
- write using accurate grammar and vocabulary and following academic style conventions
- word-process and spell accurately
- follow task instructions
- find and use the appropriate task cover sheet on Minerva.

Instructions

1. Read/Listen to the three sources your tutor gives to you.
2. Complete the list of references by word-processing the form on the next page.
3. Write a short evaluative summary **for each source** of *approximately* 8–10 sentences, which should include the following information:
    - What type of resource is this (academic/journalistic, book/article/news clip) and who is the intended audience? Is it up-to-date? Does the author appear reliable?
    - What is the main focus of the source?
    - In what ways is the source useful in answering the essay question? Is it relevant or not and why? Here you can consider

> if it describes one aspect of the topic or if it is a general overview or even which part of the essay question it might help you write – for example, does the text look at the 'lawful access' aspect of medical marijuana or does it focus on treating the symptoms of a specific illness?

What is task-based learning (TBL)?

'The role of task-based learning is to stimulate a natural desire in learners to improve their language competence by challenging them to complete meaningful tasks' (The Hong Kong Ministry of Education cited in Nunan, 2004, p14). In its truest form, TBL is very much based around 'learner-centredness' and the active involvement of the learner, which promotes 'intellectual growth' emerging from the learner's involvement in, and reflection upon, a staged task (Nunan, 2004). Based on this, TBL seems to some extent to address the needs of a typical foundation year student in that they need to improve language skills needed to negotiate a task and the skills needed to perform a task. Willis (1998, no pagination), who has been responsible for much of the most recent work on TBL, defines a task as 'a goal-oriented activity with a clear purpose'. The goal of the activity in these materials is to produce an annotated bibliography with a view to submitting something similar for assessment at a later date.

What does the TBL framework offer this group of students?

Tomlinson et al. (2001), in their evaluation of current coursebooks, found that *'the emphasis on most courses is on explicit teaching of declarative knowledge, followed by controlled or guided practice, in other words PPP'*; and this, according to Tomlinson et al. (2001), is believed to have led to a decline in skills, functions, and learner strategy development. As foundation year students need to become independent, confident learners who can discuss and negotiate with others, TBL provides them with an authentic opportunity to do this as well as giving them the confidence to approach an assessed piece of work on their own at a later stage. Structure is attended to at the end of the task once students have had an opportunity to try the task using the language skills they already possess or have negotiated with others in their group.

It was also noted by Tomlinson et al. (2001) that teaching materials often lack affective engagement and are very teacher-centred. TBL by its very nature turns PPP on its head and any instruction on grammar or any more controlled teaching only features at the end of the task cycle when students have had the opportunity to experiment and negotiate the task on their own. Working independently of a teacher is something that foundation year students will need to be able to do when they begin their undergraduate degree course. As regards affective engagement, it is hoped that allowing the students to work on a task that is part of a controversial topic and is directly related to their future studies should provide motivation, at least in the short term.

Willis has created a three-part TBL framework: 'pre-task', 'task cycle', and 'language focus' (Willis, 1996; Willis, 1998). Below, each component is explained together with how it will be used with the annotated bibliography task.

The Pre-task: This is the introduction to the topic and the task. The tutor explores the topic with the class, helps them understand the task instructions, and prepares them for the task (Willis, 1998). Useful language may be discussed, and Willis (1998) suggests that the tutor play an audio or video recording of fluent speakers doing the task they are about to perform. Dornyei (2001, cited in Ellis, 2004) stresses the fact that the task should be presented in a motivating way and that there is value in explaining the purpose of the task. This may be particularly useful for some of the foundation year cohort, many of whom come from more 'traditional' teaching backgrounds. They may need to be convinced of the merits of this more 'experimental' approach' to teaching.

In the case of these materials, the students will discuss what they know about the topic, spend time sharing ideas, and analyse the task instructions. They will have carried out some reading on the topic prior to being presented with the task and will have discussed their thoughts on it in groups and as a whole class.

The Task Cycle: According to Willis (1998), this involves doing the task in pairs/small groups, but the tutor will only monitor and not provide help with any aspect of the task. Ellis (2004) allows students to use some 'input data' from notebooks. There is also a 'planning' and 'reporting' stage where students prepare to report to the class how they did the task or alternatively swap written pieces of work and compare results. This part of the task will demand that students make use of their cognitive as well as linguistics faculties. Prabhu (1987 cited in Ellis, 2004) believes there should be a cognitive as well as linguistic aspect to tasks involving reasoning, deduction, and evaluation. Tomlinson (2003) also supports this by critiquing language teaching materials for assuming 'that learners do not want and would not gain from intellectually demanding activities whilst engaged in language learning'. For level zero students, it is vital that they are stimulated intellectually, and juggling language and challenging information is something they will have to deal with during their undergraduate studies, so it would be unrealistic to 'dumb down' the content.

In these materials during the task the students will work together to produce what they think an annotated bibliography should be according to the instructions. There will be many questions from the students at this stage! However, tutors need to stifle the desire to step in and answer them. Once they have completed this, work will be displayed around the room or sent remotely in a One Drive document *(anonymously if necessary)* and students will be asked to comment on specific aspects of each other's work, such as language, content and organisation. They will also be asked to reflect on how they worked on their own task.

Language Focus: This is *'an opportunity for explicit language instruction'* (Willis, 1996), but does not necessarily have to be tutor-led. The idea is for students to think about features of the language needed for the task such as useful phrases and common patterns. Ellis (2004) suggests also carrying out a 'repeat performance' of the task if necessary.

The students will examine certain aspects of language taken from their samples with the tutor's guidance. They will also be presented with a 'sample' task so that they can compare this to their own and other's work. Students will then be given an opportunity to try the task again, on their own, but with different input. This should help to reinforce what they have learnt and will also be a way of demonstrating how much they have learnt.

TBL: Possible problems and misconceptions

Below are some of the criticisms that could be levelled at TBL as a teaching methodology for this cohort of students and some of the ways in which these could be counteracted.

	Criticism	*Solution*
1	**Does TBL focus on 'fluency at the expense of accuracy?'**	A common misconception of TBL is that it pays scant attention to grammar. The aim of a task is for students to investigate the language themselves and to test out their own hypotheses. The language focus section can provide as little or as much attention to form as is needed. Ellis (2004) suggests opportunities for attention to form in all three phases of the cycle if the tutor wishes. *This specific cohort of students will be working in mixed language ability groups for this task. This will allow weaker students to be exposed to samples of language from stronger students with the opportunity for meaning negotiations and reformulations of utterances which contain language errors* (Ellis, 2004).
2	**Students not being keen on what they perceive as 'experimental teaching', particularly when they have an assessment at the end of it.**	Students who are used to more traditional forms of teaching, for example PPP, may need reassurance. *This cohort need to be reassured that they will be able to successfully complete their assessment. The tutor will need to explain the task cycle to the students and the pedagogical reasons behind it. There will also be an opportunity for a repeat task after the language focus component that students can perform individually using different input.*

	Criticism	Solution
3	How can students see their progress?	In this case, it would be an idea for learners to make note of the language they have learned in their notebooks and then (as noted above) to repeat the task again on their own, so they can see what they have learned from the task.
4	Tutors not being keen on the methodology behind the materials.	Tutors too may need some persuading: 'learning materials lose their value for learners if they suspect that the teacher does not value them' (Tomlinson, 2003, p18). If a tutor clearly cannot see the value in this method, then it would take very little effort to change the materials into PPP-style lessons.
5	Risks for tutors in the 'language focus' component.	TBL does require some flexibility for tutors in that the language focus section can never be fully planned for. Students may ask questions that the tutor is not prepared for or indeed cannot answer, and this may worry the more inexperienced tutor. *With this cohort, it would be acceptable for a tutor to ask the student to find out the answer for themselves for the next class.*
6	In much of the literature on TBL, the focus seems to be on speaking tasks rather than writing. How can TBL work with EAP writing tasks?	At first glance, TBL seems to be very much focused on *oral* communication rather than *written*. However, this is not the case. Willis (1996) has a section that focuses on using written tasks. A subsequent book, Willis and Willis (2007), includes a section on ESP/EAP teaching and points out that much of the discussion pre-task and during-task will involve students using the language of their specialised subject or academic language even before they have reached the written task itself.

Reflective practice

There are many ways in which we try to 'sell' the idea of autonomy to our students. First, they will not always have the support of a tutor to motivate them or tell them what they need to focus on, hence the need for training and support with this on foundation year. Second, the skills needed to be autonomous are the kind of skills employers are looking for and this benefits employability. Third, many students are required to be able to reflect on their practice and identify their strengths and weaknesses. At Leeds, we decided to incorporate reflective practice into our syllabus because it is a requirement for most students throughout their degree programmes and, more importantly, in their chosen careers. This is particularly true for those moving into healthcare careers, but we decided that, whether reflective practice is a part of their degree requirements or not, it teaches skills that are useful for undergraduate study and employment in general, such as self-evaluation, self-direction, and self-motivation. We made a reflective log part of our assessment process, which included reflective writing, but also an element that required them to work independently on their weaker areas of language or academic skills.

Why a reflective log?

The initial motivating factor for starting the log was to encourage students to read their assessment feedback. Like most tutors, we spend a lot of time writing useful feedback for students after each assessment so that they can identify the skills they need to develop and, like most tutors, we realised, with much frustration, that all students are interested in is the grade. The log was intended to consist of written entries on assessments where students would comment on the process they underwent when preparing for a particular assessment, written or oral. This would include a brief description of the task and then an evaluation of their performance, discussing the challenges during preparation, and identifying their strengths and weaknesses. Once students received their assessment feedback (minus the grade), they would be expected to comment on it. Only when they had done this would they be sent their grade. The 'carrot and stick' nature of this process may seem rather primitive, but, without it, students would not read their feedback and were missing real opportunities to develop themselves. 'Forcing' students to read and comment on feedback was, we hoped, a way of helping them to develop an appreciation of its value. As we use certain keywords and phrases from the marking rubric in our feedback, along with examples from their scripts, students become more aware of what is required of them and start to take a more mature attitude towards the grading process rather than just reacting if they think the grade they have received is unfair.

Through all of the above, we hoped that students would identify their strengths and weaknesses, comment on both and then create two or three learning objectives for themselves. They would receive help with this in the early stages, tutors would look at their objectives and help them to tweak them if necessary, as very often they would be too general or unrealistic, for example: 'I will improve my grammar' or 'I will write perfect English by the end of semester 1'. Tutors would give support by suggesting websites, university-led workshops, or books in the university Language Zone to help them achieve these objectives. Every time they carried out an activity, they would log it in the 'record of learning' and comment on how helpful it had been. We hoped that, over the academic year, this would slowly enable students to develop good learning strategies and become more adept at tackling their weak points. This activity also required a certain criticality towards their own performance and we hoped would start them on the route to becoming more mature and responsible learners.

Why assess the reflective log?

This was a little controversial with some tutors, but we felt that it encouraged motivation and, as it *is* an effort to move towards autonomy, students should be rewarded for their efforts. In our experience, if this was optional, then students would not do it. The reflective practice assessment consisted of five pre- and post-assessment written reflections plus a minimum of two activities per month towards their two or three personal learning objectives and this represented 10% of their overall grade for the study skills module. Tutors marked according to rubric. It was felt that there needed to be a balance in the way the reflections were assessed so that not too much emphasis was based on language competence, but rather on the skills associated with reflection, such as:

- acknowledging personal strengths and weaknesses
- identifying relevant targets for further development (language and/or skills) based on the strengths and weaknesses described
- understanding the usefulness of the assessment and how the skills practised might benefit students further on in their studies.

Successes and challenges

From a tutor's perspective, this assessment represented quite a lot of input in terms of providing feedback. The log was set up on the university VLE system so that tutors could at any point access each student's log and comment on the reflective writing, learning objectives, and independent learning activities; if tutors did not do this regularly then the work would mount up quite considerably, so they were encouraged to look at the logs every week. However, from the student's perspective, there were successes:

- '*I do not think I would have done these self-study tasks on my own so I think it was a good idea to make it an assessed task and I will continue to develop my skills further in my spare time. It has also helped me with becoming better at managing my time*'.
- '*I think it has helped me with my summarising skills and my vocabulary skills as well as my ability to critical think*'.
- '*I think it was helpful for me to improve my skill after the bad mark I have taken in the first semester*'.

(End of year feedback)

External examiner comments:

The reflective journal has been further developed since its introduction last year and its attempts to foster a degree of self-reflection on each learner as well as transferring the responsibility for skills development to the students themselves.

It allowed opportunities for timely intervention where necessary. Monitoring of this was sensitive and non-intrusive.

Increased participation in voluntary workshop sessions/visits to Self-Access Area.

However, not all students appreciated it, as might be expected:

It was not so good of an assignment, it was a bit hard keeping up with it, but at the same time I've learned a number of new things.

Student reactions to the reflective log could be categorised in three ways: those who took to it naturally and enjoyed writing about their experiences, those who just 'go through the motions' and do the basics required of them, and then those who see it as a 'waste of time' or do not appreciate the extra effort it involves. Students who excel at the reflective log tend to have strong intrinsic motivation and genuinely believe in its benefits, those who accept it as a necessary evil often have the extrinsic motivation of a few extra marks and those who choose not to invest usually see a mark that is just 10% of each assessment as just not worth the time and effort.

This task could be developed further for different student learning preferences. Now that technology is advanced there are options for students to record their reflections to send to tutors rather than write them. This depends on your reason for getting students to write them in the first instance, and if you want writing to be one of the skills you are assessing in addition to a student's abilities to critically reflect on their work.

Examples of student reflections and learning logs

Below is a student's reflection on the feedback for the annotated bibliography task and grade and an example from their learning log.

> Ms Nancy sent us an email containing our grade and the checked task.

> 1) It wasn't quite surprising as one of my friends told me that the word adequate in the feedback I received earlier means that my score will be between 50% and 59% and it was. I was just annoyed that I got a low mark for a lot of effort that I have put in this task. I didn't want to look in the checked task sheet for a couple of days and what I had in mind is how am I going to proceed to the degree if my grade is the lowest grade needed to be accepted by the civil engineering department. My resolve was shattered, instead of focusing on being the best and getting the highest grades. I started focusing on just getting the grade that would qualify me to proceed to the degree.

2) I didn't want to even look at any of the study skills materials on Friday. On Saturday, I had to start my essay plan as it was a compulsory part of our module and I didn't want to make the situation even worse. Later on Sunday, I opened the task sheet and I was shocked by the number of mistakes, errors, and irrelevant information that I mentioned and a lot more. Honestly, for a second, I thought that I was over-graded. I guess it was the difference in the entire marking scheme. What I realised after looking several times in my task sheet is that my main mistake was lack of checking. I didn't have enough time to check my task details after I finished it.

3) I have never faced such an experience before, usually effort was considered in checking, so when I would do a task I would rely on the fact that I have done a lot of effort in it, so I might get a good grade and this worked for quite a long time, but once I saw the corrected task, I realised that effort has nothing to do with the score or grade here in the university especially in the study skills.

4) I did put a lot of effort and time in the task, however I think that they weren't managed correctly. I focused mainly on the content, choice of words, and adding a lot of example, relevant and irrelevant. I guess that what I wrote was more of summarising and describing the article, not describing it academically for an annotated bibliography task.

5) I think that I deserve this mark, as some of my friends put less effort in the task and got higher scores, so I think I was directing myself to the wrong direction. I tried my best to keep the task title in my mind when I was writing every sentence but I guess it wasn't good enough as it has been a long time since I wrote a piece of work.

6) In the future, I plan to learn from the mistakes I made, try to keep it simple but detailed, and give a lot of importance to the final checking as I ignored it in the annotated bibliography task and saw the results myself.

Thank you

Date + Time	Sun 15 March 2015 8.13 AM
Learning objective	1. Writing a well-structured academic report.
2. Developing more logical arguments.	
Activity completed	Learning how to correctly express causes and effects.
First, I read the notes and advice on the website. Then I did the exercise to check what I've learned.	
Materials used	www.In.edu,hk/eng/rhetoric/Argumentative/Cause_And_Effect.html

Your comments about the activity	I decided to include these two learning aims in this activity because writing a report requires me to argue in a logical manner, especially in the findings section.
	I have already written my report, but this activity could be beneficial in my future writing, it might even help me alter some things in my report while proof-reading it.
	I am not sure if the used source was reliable, but the information it contains seems logical and correct to me.

Date + Time	Sunday 15 March 2015 9.01 AM
Learning objective	4. Learning how to proof-read efficiently.
Activity completed	Going through an online tutorial created by the University of Manchester regarding how to proofread efficiently.
Materials used	www.escholar.manchester.ac.uk/learning-objects/mle/proofreading/
Your comments about the activity	This activity was quite useful as it enabled me to be aware of the correct order to proof-read my work.
	It enabled me to learn new techniques to proof-read my work such as printing a hard copy and reading out loud, as it is much easier to spot mistakes while reading something out loud.

Reflective team task

Now you are at the end of this chapter, here are some questions for you and your team to discuss together:

1. How would you define *learner autonomy* for foundation year students?
2. How would you try to achieve this with your learners?
3. What have you found to be some of the barriers to achieving it? Do you think culture is one of them?
4. Do your learners take part in any kind of reflective practice? If so, what have you seen to be the benefits in terms of autonomy? If

not, would you now consider including reflective practice in your curriculum?
5   What are your views on TBL as a way of helping support autonomous learning?

References

Alrabai, F. 2017. From teacher dependency to teacher independence: a study of Saudi learners' readiness for autonomous learning of English as a Foreign Language. *Learning and Teaching in Higher Education: Gulf Perspectives,* **14** (1), pp70–97.

BALEAP. 2008. *Competency Framework for Teachers of English for Academic Purposes.* [Online]. [Accessed 16 January 2019]. Available from: www.baleap.org/wp-content/uploads/2016/04/teap-competency-framework.pdf

Benson, P. 2011. *Teaching and Researching: Autonomy.* 2nd ed. Abingdon: Routledge.

Ellis, R. 2004. *Task Based Language Learning and Teaching.* Oxford: Oxford University Press.

Littlewood, W. 1999. Defining and developing autonomy in East Asian contexts. *Applied Linguistics.* **20** (1), pp71–94.

Nunan, D. 2004. *Task-based Language Teaching.* Cambridge: Cambridge University Press.

Nunan, D. 2013. Designing and adapting materials to encourage learner autonomy. In: Benson, P. and Voller, P. eds. *Autonomy and Independence in Language Learning.* London: Routledge, pp192–204.

Palfreyman, D. 2005. Introduction: Culture and learner autonomy. In: Palfreyman, D. and Smith, R. C. eds. *Learner Autonomy Across Cultures: Language Education Perspectives.* Basingstoke: Palgrave Macmillan, pp1–19.

Pennycook, A. 2013. Cultural alternatives and autonomy. In: Benson, P. and Voller, P. *Autonomy and Independence in Language Learning.* London: Routledge, pp35–54.

Tomlinson, B. 2003. Materials evaluation. In: Tomlinson, B. ed. *Developing Materials for Language Teaching.* London: Continuum Publishing Group, pp15–37.

Tomlinson, B., Dat, B., Masuhara, H., and Rudby, R. 2001. EFL courses for adults. *ELT Journal.* **55** (1), pp80–101.

Willis, J. 1996. *A Framework for Task-Based Learning.* Essex: Longman.

Willis, J. 1998. Task-based learning – What kind of adventure? *The Language Teacher, JALT Publications.* **20** (7), [no pagination].

Willis, D and Willis, J. 2007. *Doing Task-based Teaching.* Oxford: Oxford University Press.

Index

Note: Page numbers in *italics* refer to figures.

abstracts 86
academic culture: academic integrity 10–16; communication with tutors/academic staff 2–5; expectations of students 1–2; inter-personal skills 5–10; reflective team task 18; target context, needs of 16–18
academic integrity: complexity of for students 15–16; Covid-19 impact 87–88; early intervention 15; importance of 11–12; international students 10; introductory lecture 11–12; other students work, use of 14–15; penalties for malpractice 15–16; plagiarism 114–116; reasons for academic malpractice 10–11; Turnitin 12–14
academic personal tutors (APTs) 125–126; *see also* personal tutoring
academic reading circles (ARC) 79–85
affinity bias 8–9
age/age range of students 24–25
aims, lesson 68
Alrabai, F. 139
annotations and feedback on work 26
assessment(s) 37; abstracts 86; academic integrity 87–88; academic reading circles (ARC) 79–85; assessment literacy 74, 75; awareness raising activities 70–73; benchmarking 116–117; blame culture 74; blind marking 119; cheating 114; comparability of answers 113–114; Competency Framework for Teachers of English for Academic Purposes 66; constructive alignment 66–67, *67*; Covid-19 impact 87–88; demands on teachers/tutors 98; development of 68; expectations of students 73; external examiners 120–122; feedback to students 78; formative vs summative 69; guidelines on using rubrics 113–116; learning outcomes and 66, 67; listening skills 86–87; literacy, teacher/tutors' 98–99; management 98–100; mapping to learning outcomes 67; moderation form 118; objectivity/subjectivity 99–100, *101*; oral assessment marking 119–120; pairing of teachers 96; plagiarism 114–116; preparation of students 69–73; presentations 85–86; reflective team task 88–89; rubrics, students' understanding of 70–71; rubrics, writing 100–113; samples of previous students' work 77–78; second/double marking 117–120; seminar discussions 78–79; spot marking 110–112; standardisation 117; task fulfilment 113–114; time management of students 70; timing 70; transparency in 70, 74–78; validity and reliability 98; writing consultations 71–73
attitude differences: flexibility in first weeks 2; personal tutoring 131
autonomy of students: academic reading circles (ARCs) 80; age of students 137–138; Competency Framework for Teachers of English for Academic Purposes 41, 137; concept of 138; cultural differences and 139–140; importance of 137; materials development 47; motivation 140; reflective practice by students 145–150; reflective team task 150–151; task-based learning (TBL) 140–145

Index

BALEAP Competency Framework for Teachers of English for Academic Purposes xiv–xv; academic contexts 1, 91, 115; assessment practices 66; autonomy, student 41, 137; critical thinking by students 41, 47; disciplinary differences 54; materials development 41; role in this book xiv–xv; student needs 1, 20, 50, 124; syllabus design 20, 21–22, 41; teaching practices 47, 91; text processing and production 41
Bali, M. 63
belonging opportunities through materials 50–51
benchmarking 116–117
bias 7–10
Biggs, J. 66
blame culture 74, 138
blind marking 119
British Association of Lecturers in English for Academic Purposes (BALEAP) x; Competency Framework for Teachers of English for Academic Purposes xiv–xv, 1
British Council x
buddying systems for teachers 96–98

categorisation of evidence 56–59
cause and effect language 60
Charles, M. 20–21, 24, 33, 98
cheating 114
citing *see* referencing
codes of practice 7
communication: online teaching 3; with tutors/academic staff 2–5
Competency Framework for Teachers of English for Academic Purposes xiv–xv; academic contexts 1, 91, 115; assessment practices 66; autonomy, student 41, 137; critical thinking by students 41, 47; disciplinary differences 54; materials development 41, 42; role in this book xiv–xv; student needs 1, 20, 50, 124; syllabus design 20, 21–22, 41; teaching practices 47, 91; text processing and production 41
confidentiality: disclosure of information 126, 128; personal tutoring 126, 128, 129
constructive alignment x, 66–67, *67*, 68
consultations, writing 71–73
content-based vs language split 33–34
content sharing websites 87, 114

cooperation, collaboration, team-teaching method 17
Cottrell, S. 15–16, 21, 22, 24, 42, 50, 52, 73, 75, 77, 110
Covid-19: assessment(s) 87–88; management of IFY 121–122; materials development 63–64
critical thinking 6–7, 24–25, 32, 33, 41; group discussion with roles 60; materials development 43–46, 47; wind farms topic for 43–46
criticism: constructive 6; resistance to 6
culture: autonomy of students 139–140; blame culture 74, 138; local culture 5–6; sensibilities 22–23; shock 22, 24, 73, 132–133; *see also* academic culture

dates and deadlines 38
Dawson, P. 88
deadlines 38; for staff 92
de Chazal, E. 22, 34, 42, 43, 73, 99
decolonisation of curricula 25, 62–63
deep learning 69
degree area, grouping by 32–33
degree programmes, conditions for entry into 27
disciplinary differences 54–55
disclosure of information 126, 128
disequilibrium 22, 24, 73
distracted students 25
double/second marking 117–120
Dudley-Evans, T. 17, 18
duplication of degree topics 33

Ellis, R. 143, 144
employability skills 36, 79
engagement by students 140
English as a Foreign Language (EFL) xi
English for Academic Purposes (EAP) xi
Equality and Human Rights Commission Report, Aug 2016 9
equality in mentoring system 96–97
equilibrium 22
essay mills 87, 114
evaluation of sources 68–69
expectations, management of 51–53
expectations of students 1–2, 73
external examiners: access to documentation 121; Covid-19 impact 121–122; feedback on syllabus 39; need for external moderation 120; opportunities, visits as 120–121; reports from 121

Index

face-to-face/online learning 63–64
face validity 74
feedback: reading 26; to students 78; syllabus design 38–39
flipped learning 63
focus groups of students 39
food security exercise 57–60
formative vs summative assessment(s) 69

generic vs task-specific rubrics 101–109
group bonding through materials 50
grouping: by chosen degree area 32–33; critical thinking exercise 47
group relationships and dynamics 50–51
groupwork 6

Hamp-Lyons, L. 98
healthcare, values in 54–55
healthcare codes of practice 7
Hübner, A. 75, 98, 109

implicit bias 7–10
inclusive citation 63
independent learners *see* autonomy of students
information, selection of 60, 61
integrity, academic *see* academic integrity
International English Language Testing System (IELTS) xi, 27
International Foundation Year (IFY) xi
inter-personal skills 5–10

Keating, K. 100
key information, selection of 60, 61

language focus in task-based learning 144
language level, division of groups by 26–28
lateness, flexibility regarding in first weeks 2
learning environment, prior experiences of 22–23, 73
learning outcomes (LOs) xi, 34–37, 67; assessment(s) and 66, 67
listening skills 86–87
Littlewood, W. 139
local culture 5–6
Lochtie, D. 129
Luck, C. 125, 129, 133

malpractice, academic *see* academic integrity
management of IFY: Competency Framework for Teachers of English for Academic Purposes 91; Covid-19 impact 121–122; reflective team task 122–123; staff management 91–96; team building 92; *see also* assessment(s)
Manning, A. 75, 98
marking *see* assessment(s); rubrics
materials development: appropriateness of materials 37; belonging opportunities through 50–51; Competency Framework for Teachers of English for Academic Purposes 41, 42; critical thinking 43–46; decolonisation of curricula 62–63; expectations, management of 51–53; group bonding through materials 50; group relationships and dynamics 50–51; in-house 41–42; motivation through materials 51; online/face-to-face learning 63–64; purpose of materials 42; recycling 46–50; reflective team task 64; report structure 56; study skills 42–43; values in chosen discipline 54–55
mentoring/buddying systems for teachers 96–98
minimum language requirement for entry 27
minuted team meetings 93
mitigating circumstances 130
moderation form 118
mono- or multi-lingual groups 23–24
Moon, J. 70
motivation: autonomy of students 140; through materials 51
multi- or mono-lingual groups 23–24
multi- or single-nationality cohorts 22–23

NHS Crisis project 17–18
Nunan, D. 138, 139, 142

objectivity/subjectivity in assessment(s) 99–100, 101
online/face-to-face teaching/learning 3, 63–64
open book exam – week 1 28–32
oral assessment marking 119–120

pairing of teachers 96–98
partnership 138
pastoral issues 128–129
patch writing 115
Pecorari, D. 10, 20–21, 24, 33, 98

Pennycook, A. 139
personal tutoring: academic help 131–132; academic personal tutors (APTs) 125–126; and academic tutoring 124; behaviour/attitudes, students' 131; boundaries 125, 132; competencies required for 124; Competency Framework for Teachers of English for Academic Purposes 124; confidentiality 128, 129; disclosure of information 126, 128; emotions and 125, 129; failing students 131–132; friend or mentor 132; IFY students specifically 132–133; pastoral issues 128–129; record keeping 125–126, 128; referral to other services 129; reflective team task 133–135; under 18s 126–127; safeguarding 127; special/mitigating circumstances 130; special requirements 129–130; work/personal life separation 127, 132
plagiarism: complexity of for students 15–16; early intervention 15; importance of academic integrity 11–12; international students 10; introductory lecture 11–12; managing IFY 114–116; penalties for 15–16; reasons for 10–11
politeness 3–5
pre-reading orientation 60, 61
presentations 85–86; marking 119–120; recording 119–120; rubric 101–105
pre-task in task-based learning 143
previous learning experiences and environments 2

reading lists 63
reading skills 25–26; pre-reading orientation 60, 61
reciprocity in mentoring system 97
recording of presentations 119–120
record keeping 94; personal tutoring 125–126, 128
recycling xi–xii, 36–37; evaluation of sources 68–69; materials development 46–50; wind farms topic for 46–50
referencing 36–37, 56, 57, 60, 114–115; inclusive citation 63; plagiarism, avoiding 11–12
reflective journals 95
reflective practice by students 145–150
renegade teachers 93–94
report structure 56

resistance to change 1
resistance to criticism 6
rubrics: consistency in 110; constructive language in 110; guidelines on using 113–116; matching of descriptors to tasks 112–113; spot marking 110–112; straplines 112–113; students' understanding of 70–71; task-specific vs generic 101–109; writing 100–113

safeguarding 127
samples of previous students' work 77–78
scaffolding xii, 68–69, 70
Schmitt, D. 98
Seburn, T. 79
second/double marking 117–120
self-development by students *see* autonomy of students
seminar discussions 78–79
seminars 6
shock, culture, language and academic 22, 24, 73, 132–133
single- or multi-nationality cohorts 22–23
skills development 21
skills outcomes 35–36
speaking skills 87
special/mitigating circumstances 130
spot marking 110–111
staff management: assessment management 98–100; checking on completion of tasks 93; deadlines 92; mentoring/buddying systems 96–98; minuted team meetings 93; objectivity/subjectivity in assessment(s) 99–100; pairing of teachers 96–98; record keeping 94; renegade teachers 93–94; resistance 92; strengths and weaknesses of individuals 92; supporting staff 93, 94–95; team building 91; team composition 95
standardisation 117
St John, M. J. 17, 18
straplines 112–113
subjectivity/objectivity in assessment(s) 99–100, 101
subject-specific content 16–18
summative vs formative assessment(s) 69
syllabus xii; age/age range of students 24–25; multi- or single-nationality cohorts 22–23; reflective team task 39–40

156 Index

syllabus design: Competency Framework for Teachers of English for Academic Purposes 20, 21–22, 41; content-based vs language split 33–34; cultural and religious sensibilities 22–23; dates and deadlines 38; feedback 38–39; grouping by chosen degree area 32–33; integrated approach 21; language level, division of groups by 26–28; learning objectives 21; learning outcomes 34–37; mono- or multi-lingual groups 23–24; open book exam – week 1 28–32; progression 37–38; reading skills 25–26; skills development 21; social context-based approaches 20; technology 25–26

Tang, C. 66
target context: exploration of 16; subject-specific content 16–18
task-based learning (TBL) 140–145
task cycle in task-based learning 143–144
task fulfilment 113–114
task-specific vs generic rubrics 101–109
teachers/tutors xii; assessment literacy 98–99; communication with 2–5; confidence 94; demands placed on 97–98; familiarity with norms and conventions 1; feedback on syllabus 39; mentoring/buddying systems 96–98; online teaching 3; pairing of teachers 96; record keeping by 94; renegade teachers 93–94; strengths and weaknesses of individuals 92; supporting 93, 94–95
team building 91
team composition 95
technology: annotations and feedback on work, reading 26; distracted students 25; online/face-to-face teaching/learning 3, 63–64; syllabus design 25–26
text processing and production 41
Tomlinson, B. 142, 143, 145
translation activities 24
transparency in assessment(s) 70, 74–78
Turnitin, academic integrity and 12–14
tutors/teachers xii; *see also* teachers/tutors

unconscious bias 7–10
under 18s, personal tutoring and 126–127
United Kingdom Advising and Tutoring Association xii

values in chosen discipline 54–55
video recording of presentations 119–120

washback xii, 32–33, 79
Willis, D. 143–144, 145
Willis, J. 142, 143–144, 145
wind farms topic: critical thinking 43–46; recycling 46–50
writing consultations 71–73